This book is dedicated to Helen, my wife and helpmate, and to the memory of my father; I hope I thanked him enough.

WINTER PARK PORTRAIT

The Story of Winter Park and Rollins College

"If I had my life to live over again there are not a few things that I would do differently, but I shall mention only two. First, I would cultivate my parents more than I did or most young people do. Second, I would try to fulfill in myself at the earliest moment Huxley's definition of an educated man — namely, one who knows everything about something and something about everything. I did not master anything in my life until I was over thirty years of age, and I never knew until then the power that comes to one from one's own self-respect and the respect of others when one really knows what he is talking about."

Hamilton Holt, President of Rollins College
Upon Retirement/Commencement Exercises
June 2nd, 1949

Diminutive sculpture, Byron Villwock Drive, 700 N. Interlachen

Cypress Trees, Isle of Sicily
Refectory of Alabama Lodge (1904)
"Pause friend, let beauty refresh thy spirit"
Kraft Azalea Gardens

Richard N. Campen

WINTER PARK PORTRAIT

The Story of Winter Park and Rollins College

Photographs by the Author

West Summit Press
Beachwood, Ohio
26400 George Zeiger Drive
Suite 216

Re-publication 1998 by
WINTER PARK HISTORICAL ASSOCIATION
PO Box 51
Winter Park, Florida 32790

With appreciation for support:
    Elizabeth Morse Genius Foundation
    John Tiedtke

CONTENTS

FOREWORD

I'm always pleased when someone appreciates Winter Park and its history, for this is my home town - the place where I was born and where my pioneer relatives settled over one hundred years ago.

This is a unique town with a college, a park and a golf course in its heart. Like a blossoming garden it spreads between sparkling lakes linked by fern-fringed canals. Winding streets are shaded by canopies of live oaks, many planted by my great uncle, Dr. Miller A. Henkel, Winter Park's first physician.

"Set like a gem amid the waters blue", the town is not only beautiful, but interesting as well. It offers a potpourri of cultural events: concerts and plays at Rollins College, lectures and discussions at the University Club. In the spring, there is an art festival and a Bach festival. During the Christmas season the Morse Gallery of Art shares with the community the beauty of the world's largest collection of Tiffany glass. In the park at night, they display a nativity scene and other exquisite stained-glass windows, each glittering in its own "light box". Throngs stroll among the trees listening to carols while admiring the marvelous works of art.

Winter Park is known as a "City of Homes". Richard Campen has described and photographed many of the loveliest and most historic. He is to be commended for his portrayal of this delightful town.

Dorothy Shepherd Smith

Kraft Azalea Gardens - the exedra, "Pause Friend, Let Beauty Refresh Thy Spirit" (Inscription on the exedra)

PREFACE

Winter Park Portrait: The Story of Winter Park and Rollins College is essentially an appreciation of Winter Park, its fine homes, its ambience, its history and the people who made it happen. Although the settlement of Winter Park proper commenced circa 1881, and gained considerable stimulus as a result of the activities of developers Chapman and Chase by 1885, the town was not incorporated until October, 1887 in which year the first election was held with 102 persons voting. Rollins College, for its part, was founded in 1885 - a critically important year for Winter Park as the reader will come to appreciate -, with the support of many of the same public spirited individuals who were active in the community at large.

The town and the college have, therefore, grown up together, as it were; each has drawn from and shared with the other in a symbiotic relationship. Winter Park would not today be the community of cultivated people that it is without the presence of the college. On the other hand a college without a town - and there are some - is a less interesting and vibrant place to be. This treatise reflects that interdependence.

It has not been the author's purpose to write the definitive, detailed, overly ponderous history of Winter Park with all the concommitant geneology, but rather to create an attractive, illustrated volume which would be interesting and informative to residents and, at the same time, satisfy the curiosity of the visitor and errant traveller. In the largest sense, the book-in-hand is the 'discovery' of Winter Park by an appreciator and seasoned student of architectural history - with emphasis upon its architecture and ambience.

Winter Park, beyond being the home of Rollins College and a center of fine shops, is a city of distinctive homes built in the century between 1885 and 1985. Since today its population has increased five-fold from the 4,715 residents of 1940, the majority of these homes have been built in the post World War II years. An important objective of the book is the visual portrayal and description of these residences with particular emphasis on those in being before the onset of World War II.

Unlike many of the well-known coastal cities in Florida - and they are the only ones with which Winter Park can be compared - apartment and condominium living is here the exception. The multiple dwellings of Winter Park - none of them high-rise in the truest sense - could almost be counted on the fingers of both hands. Blessed with a beautiful chain of lakes responsible for her many, lovely, curving streets; blessed with a climate favorable to the growth of live oaks and other deciduous trees as well as citrus and palms of various types - the residential sections of Winter Park stand comparison, in Florida, only with Palm Beach, Naples and perhaps one or two other communities.

The author wishes to acknowledge the assistance given by the following: Gertrude F. LaFramboise who guided him through the archival resources of Rollin's Olin Library and to the Library for permission to reproduce many historic photos; Byron Villwock, who chauffeured him around the many nooks and crannies of Winter Park; Jean Shannon, octogenarian, with the clearest recollections of by-gone days in Winter Park; Flora Twatchman, who kindly opened the doors of 'Eastbank'- the Comstock-Harris house; Mr. and Mrs. Roger Holler who graciously permitted the interior photographing of 'Casa Feliz', likewise Ms. Kathy Taylor owner of the lovely, mid 1920's residence located at 1411 Via Tuscany and Dr. and Mrs. Charles Curry current owners of the former A.G. Bush estate, and finally wishes to acknowledge, with gratitude, a debt to Dorothy Shepherd Smith, life-long resident of Winter Park, a Rollins College graduate and historian, who reviewed the manuscript and was otherwise most helpful.

Richard N. Campen
August 1, 1987

Aerial perspective of Winter Park (1888)

As it might have looked in David Mizell's time.

THE WINTER PARK STORY

DAVID MIZELL - the first settler
TRAVEL TO WINTER PARK - a century ago

All accounts credit David Mizell as being the first white man to settle in the area which we now know as Winter Park. He came overland with his family in 1858 from Alachua County, of which Gainesville is now the seat, to a place known as Osceola located on an old Indian trail which skirted the eastern shore of Lake Osceola. Here he built a log cabin near what is now the intersection of Phelps and Mizell Avenues and engaged primarily in growing cotton, livestock, and vegetables necessary to sustain himself and his family which ultimately included ten children.

At that time, thirteen years after Florida was admitted to the Union, three years before she seceded therefrom at the outset of the Civil War, Florida was largely a trackless wilderness. The region traversed by Mizell had been sparsely inhabited by the Seminole Indians. However, under Chief Osceola the Indians, little more than fifteen years earlier, had lost the Second Seminole War (1835-1842) when resisting the Federal Government's attempts to resettle them in the Oklahoma Territory and were forced to leave: i.e. all but perhaps 150 who fled to the Everglades. This residual nucleus of the tribe has increased in population ten-fold or more to our time. Two of the numerous lakes within and surrounding Winter Park today are named after the pioneer, Mizell, and the Indian Chief, Osceola.

The more conventional approach to central Florida during the third quarter of the nineteenth century and beyond was via the St. Johns River which, along with a tributary, the Oklawaha, were principal arteries to the interior. For the insight to be gained into the Florida condition in the decades preceding the founding of Winter Park and for some years thereafter, let us follow the fictitious journey of a traveller coming this way in Mizell's time. He would, of necessity, have paddled as far as Mellonville, then a trading post on the south shore of Lake Monroe, near the present location of Sanford, and then proceeded overland for the balance of his journey to lake district destinations.

En route, without doubt, our mythical traveller would have docked at Palatka which, while very small in 1858, was to become a major port-of-call for all steamers plying the river - as well as a final destination for many "winter rusticators" from the north. The inauguration of the Putnam House there in 1879 was honored by the presence of Pres. Ullysses S. Grant who shortly thereafter drove the first spike in the South Florida Railroad originating at Sanford. By October of 1880 the 24 mile stretch through the future site of Winter Park to Orlando had been completed and, beginning in November of that year, two trains daily made the run between Sanford and Orlando in the remarkable time of one hour and forty minutes.

In Palatka our traveller would have seen St. Marks Episcopal Church, erected in 1854, which still stands to this day. This venerable and captivating little building is of board and batten construction with an engaged "campanile" at its right, front corner. A historical marker before the church notes that "During the Civil War St. Marks was used as a barracks by Federal troops and suffered considerable damage. After the War the Church served as the missionary center for the Episcopal Church in the St. Johns valley."

Also in Palatka, he would have been impressed with the stately Bronson-Mulholland House built in 1854. With a broad porch and balustraded balcony encircling its south and east facades, it is the epitome of the ante-bellum southern plantation house - quite comparable to the Gamble Mansion near Bradenton. Both are today museums interpretive of the life-styles and decorative arts of their time. A short distance up-river from Palatka the Oklawaha River branches off from the St. Johns in a generally southwestward direction to Silver Springs which also was to become a popular destination.

Eventually, the lively river traffic was handled by small, paddle-wheel steamers. The jumping-off point was Jacksonville which by 1870 boasted a population of over 4,000. By the early 1880's, when Winter Park's development was just getting under way, Jacksonville's population had soared to over 15,000. It then had approximately forty

Bronson-Mulholland House (1854)

St. Marks Episcopal Church, Palatka (1854)

The St. James Hotel (1869) Jacksonville

Pulsifer Place Marker, honoring Royal MacIntosh Pulsifer

hotels and many boarding houses which are said to have entertained as many as 75,000 winter visitors in the course of a season.

The St. James, known as the "Fifth Avenue Hotel of Florida" was the most popular and attractively appointed of the Jacksonville hotels. Entirely of wood construction, three stories in height, it was built in 1869. From the roof of its ground-floor veranda, giant columns extended through two floors to its bracketted cornice. Scrollwork, popular at the time with the introduction of the band saw, decorated the column capitals and spaces between. This popular and comparatively elegant hotel was lost, as unfortunately was so often the case with large wooden hotels of the period, to a fire in 1891.

Carlton W. Tebeau in his "History of Florida" sheds additional light on the Florida condition in these early years writing as follows:

"William Cullen Bryant who had been in Florida in 1843, returned thirty years later and reported on the local scene to the New York Evening Post. Palatka, he wrote, was still largely a forest. Jacksonville was thriving, with four thousand people and two new hotels, both full. St. Augustine had some new homes and two new hotels, with orange trees growing everywhere. The northern invasion was under way.........He visited Green Cove Springs and went up the Oklawaha to Silver Springs and Ocala. Two hotels at Silver Springs, one at Magnolia, and two at Palatka were full and though accommodations at St. Augustine had been doubled over the previous year, they were also full. He predicted a rosy future for the Sunshine State".)

PULSIFER PLACE

In honor of Royal MacIntosh Pulsifer (1843 - 1888) Mayor of Newton, Mass.; Publisher-owner of the Boston Herald. Pres. of the first Railroad across Florida connecting St. Johns River with Tampa Bay. Aided founders of Winter Park.

From the above it may be seen that Jacksonville, in particular, but also Magnolia Springs and Green Cove Springs as well as St. Augustine, were prime destinations in the 1870's for northerners wishing, then as now, to escape winter's bleak days and penetrating chill. Against this background it is not at all surprising that Loring Chase of Chicago in 1881 came to the area which would become Winter Park - no doubt via the St. Johns River route which we have just vicariously traversed - and shortly, in partnership with his friend Oliver Chapman, purchased 600 acres with dreams of establishing yet another winter community in an even more southerly, ingratiating climate.

By this time Captain Jacob Brock had founded the town of Enterprise on the north shore of Lake Monroe and there built the renouned Brock House to accommodate travellers and sportsmen - for word of the great fishing thereabouts had spread far and wide. Brock also operated steamers on the Jacksonville-Enterprise route. Additionally, in 1871, Henry L. Sanford, Lincoln's ambassador to Belgium, had purchased a tremendous tract of 12,000 acres near the site of Mellonville - across the Lake from Enterprise - and laid out Sanford, Florida. Sanford was instrumental in attracting many Swedes and Englishmen to the area who, at this time, were fleeing adverse economic conditions in their homelands. One such person was J. C. Stovin who, later in Winter Park became a successful citrus grower and, in 1882, a contributor to the building of the original railroad station in Winter Park. This post Civil War period marked the beginning of the development of Florida which, except for several economic and weather related interruptions, has continued unabated ever since.

(Refer to map on page 112)

FISH, FOWL AND FUN

— IN —

FLORIDA, U. S. A.

DE BARY AND PEOPLE'S LINE STEAMERS

on St. Johns River.

DAILY SERVICE BETWEEN

JACKSONVILLE, TOCOI, PALATKA, ROLLESTON, WELAKA, ASTOR, DeLAND LANDING, BLUE SPRINGS, SANFORD AND ENTERPRISE,

and all landings on St. Johns river. Iron and steel hulls; low pressure engines. Strictly first-class in every particular. Foremost and famous for the safety, speed and regularity of schedules.

CONNECTIONS AT JACKSONVILLE WITH RAILROAD AND STEAMSHIP LINES, DIVERGING

at Tocoi, with St. Johns Railway for St. Augustine; at Palatka, with Florida Southern Railway for Gainesville, Micanopy, Ocala, Silver Springs, Leesburg, Brooksville, and stations on Charlotte Harbor Division, also with Palatka and St. Augustine Railway; at Rolleston, with St. Johns and Halifax Railway for Ormond, Daytona, and landings on Halifax river; at Astor, with the St. Johns and Eustis Division Florida Southern Railway for Kismet, Altoona, Ravenswood, Ft. Mason, Eustis, Tavares, Lane Park and landings on Lakes Harris, Eustis and Griffin; at DeLand Landing, with Railway for DeLand; at Blue Springs, with Blue Springs, Orange City and Atlantic Railway for Orange City, Lake Helen, New Smyrna, and landings on Halifax and Hillsborough rivers; at Sanford, with South Florida Railroad for stations thereon and its connections for points on the Gulf of Mexico, Key West and Havana; at Enterprise, with St. Johns, Atlantic and Indian River Railroad for Titusville, Rock Ledge, and landings on Indian river.

W. M. DAVIDSON,
General Traffic Agent
People's Line.

D. H. ELLIOTT,
Gen. Frt. & Pass. Agt.
DeBary Line.

JACKSONVILLE, FLA.
58

'Steamer' plying the St. Johns Waterway (1880's)

Oliver Chapman (left), Loring Chase (right)

THE ORIGINS OF WINTER PARK

Apart from David Mizell and a handful of early settlers, the real development of Winter Park commenced with the arrival of Loring A. Chase early in the year 1881. At this time Chase was 42 years of age, having been born on the 21st of August, 1839 in Nashua, New Hampshire. His mother and father had both died by the time he was two years old so he was sent to live with an aunt and uncle in Canton, Mass. where, upon his uncle's death while still a boy, he took charge of a grocery store. Eventually, he went to Boston and secured a job as a bookkeeper. In 1865, after having served a nine month stint with a Massachusetts regiment in North Carolina - beckoned by the promise of opportunities in the West - he took a position with the First National Bank of Chicago. He attended a business school while residing in Chicago and endured the Great Chicago fire of 1871. In 1880 his doctor advised him to go south to alleviate violent headaches attributed to catarrh and bronchitis. He left for Florida with the definite idea of engaging in development.

Upon arriving in central Florida Chase, at first, is said to have made his way, by means of a small steamer, from Sanford on Lake Monroe to the vicinity of Titusville and thence, again by boat, to the inter-coastal community of Rockledge. Unimpressed with the Indian River region, he returned to Sanford where Mr. J. E. Ingraham, Agent for General Sanford's vast land holdings, attempted unsuccessfully to interest him in that area. This office then alerted Chase to property owned by a Mr. B. R. Swoope bordering Lakes Maitland and Osceola. He was immediately impressed upon inspection of the property, but hesitated to undertake alone the development plans he had in mind for a beautiful community of winter homes for wealthy northerners. The climate appears to have completely cured him of his bronchial discomfort.

Chase seems to have known that an old friend, Oliver E. Chapman also of Canton, Mass., was visiting a brother-in-law in Florida, but did not have a clue as to his exact where-abouts. When advised of the brother-in-law's name, the land agent with whom Chase was working recalled that there was such a party in Sorrento - some twenty odd miles distant - which, to that time, had attracted four or five homesteaders. An exchange of telegraph messages verified that this party was, indeed, the one being visited by Chapman and his invalid wife. The two men met in Sanford the very next day.

Together Loring A. Chase and Oliver E. Chapman inspected the Swoope and adjoining properties. Sharing their enthusiasm for the sites, they jointly purchased three homesteads, comprising six hundred acres, for approximately $13,000 - receiving the deeds to same on July 1, 1881. Chapman moved his family from Sorrento to Maitland where he took up residence in a house owned by Dr. Clement C. Haskell whose brother, an owner of The Boston Herald, was instrumental in the establishment of the South Florida Railroad. Commuting daily that summer to their property which was then a wilderness studded with tall pine trees and a few abandoned cabins, the two boyhood friends from Canton, Mass. hired Samuel A. Robinson for a fee of $50 to survey their holdings and laid out a town which, following much soul-searching, they appropriately named Winter Park.

Their selection of this land-of-lakes as the site for the residential community and resort hotel which they envisioned was a particularly fortunate one: the first consideration was, of course, the beauty of the region with its tall, virgin pines (now mostly gone) and clear, pristine lakes. Its elevation, 92 feet above the level of Lake Monroe, was considered desirable from the standpoint of health, good drainage and dryness. Furthermore, it was not far from Sanford - the head of navigation on the St. Johns waterway and was in the path of the South Florida Railroad then being pushed through from Sanford to Orlando.

Chapman and Chase had the foresight to plan (we emphasize "plan") their new haven in the south thereby avoiding the more usual topsy-turvy growth which might otherwise have taken place. They provided, in their plan, for a central park bisected by a central boulevard; they provided three lake-front sites for resort hotels: one at the eastern

Park Avenue in 1890 - aspect south

The Rogers House (1882)

Original Winter Park RR Station (1882)

The Rogers House with 1888 Addition

extremity of New England Avenue which would be occupied by the famed Seminole Hotel, a large one immediately south of Webster Avenue's eastern extremity - eventually occupied by The Osceola Inn, and one on a portion of the site now occupied by Rollins College.

Very early, a sizeable lot immediately south of The Boulevard between Interlachen Avenue and Lake Osceola was made available to Alfred E. Rogers and his wife, who were camping at Osceola, with the provision that they erect and operate a hotel thereon. A business section was designated; also an area was set aside for blacks. The Rogers House, which opened for business in April of 1882, was the second structure to be built in Winter Park following the railroad station by exactly one month.

From 1881 to 1885 Chase and Chapman advertised the new town, opened up streets, planted orange trees, built a store, town hall and some cottages. The presence of the South Florida Railroad, financed by the R. M. Pulsifer & Co. of Boston, ultimately to run from Sanford to Tampa, certainly worked in their favor. Since the railroad would not undertake to build a Winter Park station, realizing its importance to the development of the community, it was then privately subscribed "by the undersigned who agree(d) to pay the amounts set against their names for the purpose of building a depot."

Chase and Chapman	$150.00
Dr. Ira Geer	50.00
John R. Mizell	25.00
Lewis Lawrence	100.00
J.C. Stovin	50.00
W.C. Comstock	100.00
Wilson Phelps	25.00
Conway	50.00
R.R. Thayer	8.00
Total	$758.00

Originally, it was thought by the author that this far sighted philanthropy accounted for the not inconsiderable "detour" and curve of the railroad as it passes through Winter Park, until it was pointed out that the RR between Sanford and Orlando was completed by October 1, 1880 whereas the station was not built until March 18, 1882. To this day there is no valid explanation as to why the railroad made this deviation from the straight-away.

This original Winter Park station, located across the tracks from the present, contemporary station, was of wood, frame construction in what has become known as the "stick style". In true depot design, its concave roof overhung the ground platform so as to shelter waiting passengers. Until the end of World War II, with the explosion of civil aviation and the national highway system following thereafter, the railroad provided the principal transportation link between Winter Park, Rollins College and the rest of the world.

The Rogers House opened for business in April, 1882 with a gala dinner party attended by seventeen guests. The lot given to the Rogers by Chapman and Chase was on the "Boulevard" (now Morse Boulevard) presently occupied by The Cloisters Apartments. It was of "four square" construction, three floors in height, with porches on all floors under a nearly flat roof. Its original 20 - 30 chambers were doubled in number by an 1888 addition which included a Mansard-capped element at its right rear corner imparting something of the Italian villa style to its silhouette. A broad hall extended through the length of the establishment with two attractive parlors to its left.

The Rogers House served under the name of its original proprietors for 22 years until purchased by Charles Hosmer Morse for $7,000 in 1904 when it was completely overhauled and reopened on the 26th of April in that year as The Seminole Inn. It was a cozy place which from the time that it opened attracted many of Winter Park's most distinguished visitors among whom were: Mr. and Mrs. Franklin Fairbanks, Mr. and Mrs. Francis Knowles, Mr. and Mrs. Charles Hosmer Morse. Its charm was its small size and elite clientele. Mr. Rogers advertised:

Peleg Peckham's Cottage viewed from Seminole Hotel (c. 1887)

Park Avenue c. 1888; the Henkel Block

16

Above - Olin Library (1985), Rollins College
Below - Rendezvous - Kraft Azalea Gardens

Above - Park Avenue - Art Festival, 1987
Below - Art Festival 'takes over' Central Park

17

"Bathrooms, hot and cold running water and closets on each floor. Guest rooms and furnishings second to none in the country; excellent table: Rates - $2.00, $2.50 and $3.00 per day; $10.00 to $17.00 per week. Located on beautiful Lake Osceola 18 miles south of Sanford on the South Florida Railroad; three minutes walk from the depot - surrounded by piney woods and orange groves; light, airy rooms commanding magnificent lake views, pure spring water, lake full of fish. You will not be disappointed."

By the mid 1880's word about Winter Park, as being among the most beautiful and healthful spots in all of Florida, had spread far and wide. This was due, in no small part, to Loring Chase's enthusiasm and salesmanship. He spent a good part of each winter in Jacksonville extolling the glories of Winter Park to everyone within ear-shot. Oliver Chapman, for his part, would then show them about in a horse-drawn buckboard. The visit of Pres. Chester Arthur to Winter Park in April of 1883 accompanied by William E. Chandler, Secretary of War, and other notables, both enhanced its reputation and added momentum to its development. The president came at the invitation of Judge Lewis H. Lawrence, millionaire boot and shoe manufacturer from Utica, New York who in 1875 had purchased a ten acre tract bordering the south shore of Lake Maitland and in 1882 built the house now identified as number 1300 Summerland Avenue.

In promoting Winter Park and other Florida communities during these years a great deal of emphasis was placed on the healthful climate. This is why Loring Chase had come to the region in the first instance; why Dr. Miller A. Henkel came in 1884 with a wife failing from tuberculosis - a national scourage following the Civil War; why the legendary Henry Flagler came to Jacksonville in the early 1880's, and why Edward H. Brewer, a wealthy manufacturer of carriage accessories in Cortland, New York, came to Winter Park in 1895 and eventually built one of its most impressive "cottages", "the Palms", on land formerly owned by Alonzo Rollins on the eastern shore of Lake Osceola.

Dr. Henry Foster, operator of a convalescent home in Clifton Springs, New York is quoted, at the time, as saying of Winter Park: "No locality is more healthful or more beautiful." Mrs. Mary J. Holmes, an authoress writes (1886-87): "This is my seventh winter in Florida and having visited nearly all of the points of interest in the State, I can conscientiously say that for beauty of situation and purity of atmosphere Winter Park excells them all. Standing as it does nearly 100' above the sea-level of the St. Johns River, it is wholly free of dampness and malaria, while the surrounding scenery is unrivaled for beauty and variety."

Harriet Beecher Stowe (1811-1896), author of "Uncle Tom's Cabin" said, "I think that every rich man or woman should have a winter home in Florida for pleasure and for health. Every man in moderate circumstance should have such a home for profit." We wish to emphasize that in the 1880's and 1890's health was a great motivating factor leading people to come to Florida; today, to a far greater extent, people come for fun and recreation.

First Commercial Building, Park Avenue at Morse Blvd.

FORMATION OF THE WINTER PARK CO. THE SEMINOLE HOTEL IS BUILT.

The Chapman-Chase partnership came to an end early in 1885 when Chapman sold his interest to Chase for $40,000. Immediately thereafter, the Winter Park Company was organized and chartered by the State, with capital stock of $300,000, to continue with the promotion and development of Winter Park. Frederick W. Lyman of Minneapolis was elected president; Franklin Fairbanks of St. Johnsbury, Vt. vice-president; F. G. Webster of Kidder-Peabody, New York City, treasurer and Loring Chase, secretary. Judge J. F. Welborne of Winter Park, William C. Comstock and Alonzo W, Rollins, both of Chicago, were elected directors. (There is some disagreement among several sources as to the officer assignments cited above). All of these men were important, early "movers and shakers" of Winter Park who will figure prominently in all phases of its development as our story unfolds.

The initial meeting of the Company's board was held on the 16th of April in 1885. Loring Chase subscribed for 2,990 shares backed by real estate pledged to the company. Lyman subscribed for 74 shares, Comstock for 75, Rollins for 112, Lawrence for 25, Knowles for 179, J. S. Capen for 14 and Samuel Capen for 13. Six days after incorporation, on April 22nd, the Company authorized the president and secretary to contract for the building of a 150 room hotel, to arrange for a loan of $50,000, and to hire W.E. Forbes as manager at an annual salary of $1,200.

Thus, the die was cast for the construction of the fabled Seminole Hotel which was to become the largest such establishment south of Jacksonville; not, however, before an additional building loan of $150,000 was secured from director Francis Knowles. Loring Chase was the project manager; McGuire & MacDonald, builders of the Magnolia Hotel at Magnolia, Florida and the San Marcos in St. Augustine, were appointed contractors. It boggles the mind that a building project of this dimension could have been completed, and opened for business, on Janaury 1, 1886 in time to enjoy virtually the entire winter season as stated in Blackman's "History of Orange County" and elsewhere.

"THE SEMINOLE," WINTER PARK, FLORIDA.
—Accomodations for 400 Guests.—

Two hundred men were on the job most of the time and there is no doubt that this huge facility was, indeed, built and fitted out between April 22nd and December 31, 1885. A sumptuous banquet and ball were held the very next day to celebrate the gala opening. It is said that during the ensuing three months the Seminole registered 2,300 guests - a prodigious figure. Again, whatever the number, it attests to the interest in Florida and the super promotional job done by Chapman, Chase and The Winter Park Company.

The Seminole was located on Lot #522 at the eastern extremity of New England Ave. - one of those originally designated as a hotel site - with spacious grounds overlooking Lake Osceola. It was five floors in height under a Mansard roof perforated by numerous dormers. The structure was very much in style in that the Mansard roof in America was a comparatively new innovation, having been employed for the very first time on these shores by architect John Renwick at what is now the Renwick Gallery (1859 - 1861) in Washington, D. C.. (Renwick's most famous work is New York's St. Patrick Cathedral). At this very time, i.e. the 1880's, dozens of courthouses employing the Mansard roof were being built in the rapidly developing states of Ohio, Indiana and Illinois.

The Seminole's ground floor veranda, supported by bracketted columns, wrapped around at least two sides of the elongated hotel which encompassed twenty-seven window bays across its principal facade. A portico at the center of this long veranda, fronting New England Avenue, received guests escorted from the RR station in a horse-drawn "street-car". From a roof-top belvedere guests enjoyed wonderful views across Lakes Osceola and Virginia. The dining-room had dimensions of 42' x 100'; the total length of the so-called "piazza", said to have been 567 feet and variously 16' to 24' in width, suggests that it encircled most of the structure. The Seminole was a quite modern and sophisticated building for its time; it is difficult to believe that it could have been achieved without an architect or, at least, the skill of very knowledgeable master builders which in this instance appears certainly to have been the team of McGuire and MacDonald.

This thoroughly modern hotel accommodated 400 guests; it was heated by steam throughout and lighted by gas. It had an elevator, electric service bells, fire alarm system, an approved fire escape, hot and cold baths and what were termed "suadaria" (steam baths). It offered fresh vegetables from neighboring gardens, fruits and berries from local groves and shrubberies. For recreation, aside from strolling on the veranda, one could engage in billards or bowling, croquet or tennis, also bathing or rowing on the lakes; good saddle and carriage horses were available. The season ran only from January 1st to April 10.

The Seminole entertained many famous people over the years including Charles F. Crocker of San Francisco, George M. Pullman, George Westinghouse, Hamilton Disston, Edward Pierrepont, the Duke of Sutherland and the Honorable S. Plimsoll of England, but none was received more enthusiastically than Pres. Grover Cleveland who arrived February 24, 1888 accompanied by Col. Daniel Lamont, his private secretary, William C. Whitney and their wives along with several senators. Hundreds of guests greeted the President and participated in a brilliant reception staged in his honor.

In April of 1886 Loring Chase sold his commanding interest in the Winter Park Co. to Francis B. Knowles and retired feeling that he had "money enough to last me while I live." Thus in five short years Chapman and Chase realized their fondest dreams when investing the $13,000 in 1881. Loring Chase remained a resident of Winter Park until his death in August of 1906. His historical inclinations prompted him to keep a scrapbook of newspaper clippings, letters and memorabilia of these years which today comprises the primary source of information relating to the founding and development of Winter Park to 1906. Very few communities are fortunate to have such a complete record which, it should be noted, has been indexed and often transcribed, by Dorothy Shepherd Smith.

It is interesting to compare the vacation customs and expectations of the 1880's with those of today—100 years later. Most vacationers who come to Florida today want to be near a beach and a golf course; they demand amenities such as fashionable shops and gourmet restaurants. Winter Park in the 1880's offered none of these. The first golf course, opened in 1899, consisted of nine holes located between Lyman Avenue on the north and Holt on the south, between Interlachen and New York Avenues - east and west. Sheep were employed to keep the scrubby grass under control. This course was closed in 1912. One hundred years ago there was not a single paved street or sidewalk in Winter Park.

Park Avenue, partially lined on one side with two-story, frame, building blocks, had the appearance of a western cow-town where one could shop for medicine, hardware items, dry goods and little more. There was not a single restaurant in town aside from the dining-rooms in the hotels. Billards, pool and croquet, so popular then, are uncommon today, as are also, largely, the inland resort hotel as exemplified by the Seminole - though it must be acknowledged that Disneyland and Epcot have reversed this condition.

WHO WERE THESE PIONEERS?

FRANCIS B. KNOWLES

Francis Bangs Knowles, initially director - subsequently owner of the Seminole Hotel, was born in Hardwick, Mass. on November 29, 1823. Following education at the Leicester Academy, he taught school briefly in Dana, Massachusetts and subsequently at Gloversville, New York. There, in 1845, he entered into the manufacturing of gloves and, before the year was out, married a Gloversville girl who bore him two children. The firm sold gloves to the Union army during 1861-62. In March of 1862 he joined his brother who was engaged in manufacturing looms and steam pumps in Warren, Mass. This business was moved to Worcester, Mass. in 1866 where, the first Mrs. Knowles having passed away the previous year, he remarried and fathered three additional children - one of these being Frances W. Knowles who, as we shall shortly see, following in her father's footsteps, became a great benefactor of Rollins College.

Knowles made his first trip to Florida in the winter of 1883 at the age of 60 when, in the course of his travels, he encountered an old friend, Col. Franklin Fairbanks, while steaming up the Oklawaha River in the vicinity of Silver Springs. It is quite likely that at this time he also visited Winter Park. At any rate, Fairbanks who had first come to Winter Park a year or two earlier, and had interests there, certainly made Knowles aware of this developing community.

In 1884 the Knowles Loom Works was incorporated with Francis B. Knowles as President. The company prospered greatly becoming one of the largest industrial organizations in New England; its plants covered five acres. As we have seen, by 1885 Knowles was back in Florida where he became a director of the Winter Park Company and, with the purchase of Loring Chase's interests, its largest stockholder.

In the comparatively few years that followed, Francis B. Knowles veritably became "Mr. Winter Park". He figured importantly in the founding of Rollins College in 1885 and became a member of its first Board of Trustees. He personally financed Knowles Hall - the College's first

building which was completed early in 1886. We have seen that he loaned $150,000 towards the building of the Seminole Hotel; this involvement resulted in his becoming its largest single stockholder, if not the sole owner upon the withdrawal of Chapman and Chase. He assumed control of the Orlando and Winter Park RR. - the "Dinky Line" - and saw that it was completed. In 1890 he gave the funds for the construction of Knowles Public School in Winter Park. The cottage which he built for himself in 1888 at 231 Interlachen Avenue, subsequently acquired by Charles Hosmer Morse in 1904 and named "Osceola Lodge", still exists. It is one of a half dozen landmarks designated by the City of Winter Park.

Francis Bangs Knowles passed away in Washington, D. C. on the 15th of May, 1890 at age 67 and thereafter was interred in Worcester, Mass.. He made a mighty impact on the emerging village of Winter Park in the comparatively few winter seasons that he spent there. The following statement made by Mr. J. S. Capen, a close associate of Knowles as Secretary of the Winter Park Co., sheds light on his character:

> As an employer he was kind and thoughtful. His interests in the growth of the town were zealously looked after and everything done to make this the pretty city that it is. Mr Knowles was genial and affable, and both he and Mrs. Knowles were a great addition to the social life of the fast growing city. Himself an earnest and consistent Congregationalist, he was broad-minded and tolerant, and an appeal to him for help in religious and charitable matters met with a generous response as soon as he knew that the cause was worthy..."

It was also said of him: "Mr. Knowles bore his prosperity modestly. The great bulk of his income has been dispensed to charities of which the public never had an inkling and he chose that they should not."

FREDERICK WOLCOTT LYMAN

Frederick Wolcott Lyman, born in Plymouth, Connecticut on the 18th of June, 1849, came from a well known, even illustrious, Connecticut family. His maternal grandfather, General Jedediah Huntington, was a close friend and aid to Gen. Washington during the Revolutionary War. Following

The "Dinky Station"

The locomotive "F.B. Knowles"

education in the public schools, Lyman attended the Gunnery School in Washington, Conn. Even as Loring Chase had done, Lyman heeded the dictum of Horace Greeley "Go west, young man, go west", for the year 1871 finds him engaged in business in Minneapolis, Minn. He obviously was very successful for he became a director of several banks and ultimately a trustee of several colleges including Pomona College at Clarement, California, the Chicago Theological Seminary and Rollins in Winter Park.

Lyman appears first to have come to Winter Park in the Spring of 1882 when only 33 years of age. Thereafter, he spent many winters amidst its lakes and pine woods. Obviously an achiever and a "doer", he became deeply involved in the development of the community, as well as the founding of the Congregational Church and Rollins College. Although his financial interest in the Winter Park Company was much smaller than Chase's or Chapman's, he became the first president of its Board of Directors. As such, he was certainly very much involved with the planning and the building of the Seminole Hotel. The Lyman house in Winter Park was located on the Boulevard - now Morse Blvd. - overlooking Lake Osceola opposite the Rogers Inn. It was razed not so many years ago to make way for Whispering Waters condominium. After being vacated by the Lymans, however, it was occupied by Dr. and Mrs. William F. Blackman President of Rollins College between 1902 and 1915 and for a time thereafter was operated as the Green Gables Tea Room. Its final occupants, to 1945, were Walter and Louise Schultz of whom we shall learn more later on.

As early as 1883 Lyman is said to have been the first person to suggest the founding of a college in Winter Park and he subsequently played an active role in its realization. In addition to serving as a trustee for many years, he gave Rollins College its first gymnasium in 1890. Later in life Lyman took up residence in Pasadena, California where he was still alive in 1927 at which time he would have been seventy-eight years of age. Although distant, having played such an important role in its development, he surely always had a warm spot in his heart for Winter Park and its college.

COLONEL FRANKLIN FAIRBANKS

Colonel Fairbanks was born in St. Johnsbury, Vermont on June 28, 1828. At age 18 he entered the large scale works established by his father and uncles. He was admitted to partnership in 1856 at age 28 and eventually became president in 1888. In addition, he was, in the course of his life, both an officer and director of a number of mining, manufacturing, banking and telegraph enterprises. He represented his hometown in the Vermont legislature in 1870-72 and was elected speaker of the House in 1872. Dartmouth College conferred an honoroary degree upon him in 1877.

Fairbanks first came to Winter Park in 1881-82 in company with his friend and business associate Charles Hosmer Morse also a native son of St. Johnsbury. At this very time Mssrs. Chapman and Chase were busily engaged in laying out and alloting their recently acquired land holdings. Fairbanks and Morse each purchased lots on Interlachen Avenue fronting Lake Osceola. This was Morse's first stake in what was ultimately to become his immense land holdings with the purchase of the Knowles interests in 1904. Colonel Fairbanks became Vice President of The Winter Park Company upon its organization in 1885. He was an officer as well as one of the original stockholders in the Seminole Hotel and continued as such beyond 1890. Additionally, he was a benefactor and charter trustee of Rollins College from its founding in 1885 until his death in 1895.

Throughout his life Fairbanks was deeply interested in church work; he served as a member of the International Sunday School Lesson Committee and was Superintendent of the St. Johnsbury Sunday School for thrity years. The breadth of his interests in shown in his support of a Museum of Natural Science and donation of an Athenaeum in Undercliffe, Vermont. Winter Park was most fortunate to have attracted men of this calibre in its formative years; it still does.

Francis Bangs Knowles (1823 - 1890)

Col. Franklin Fairbanks (1828 - 1895)

The Seminole Hotel (1886 - 1902)

23

JAMES SEYMOUR CAPEN

James S. Capen, an early settler, made important contributions to Winter Park during his residency from July of 1884 until the great freeze of 1895. With the withdrawal of Loring Chase in April of 1886, he became Secretary of the Winter Park Company. Capen first came to Winter Park at the urging of Loring Chase. They had met, as fellow students, in the State Normal School in Bloomington, Illinois. Chase had, in fact, boarded in the Capen home in Bloomington while attending the School and had originally come to Florida from the Capen home.

Capen's principal business in Winter Park was planting and caring for orange groves; however, he also dealt in real estate. His office occupied one of the five store spaces in the Henkel Block (1886) - the grandest building in town - located at the northeast corner of Park and New England Avenues, a lot now occupied by the Barnett Bank. As a promoter of the Orlando and Winter Park Railroad, he attended the ground-breaking of the "Dinky" station on April 4, 1887. Additionally, he was an officer of the Winter Park Improvement Society upon its founding in 1890.

Capen was born in Union Springs, Cayuga County, New York on October 18, 1852. His French Huguenot Ancestors, driven from France and England, came to America in 1630. The family name was changed from Campinne to Capen. The Capens, too, were caught up in the westward movement; James received his education in the public schools of Blommington, Illinois, then, as has been noted, at the State Normal School there. His interest in Florida stimulated by Loring Chase, he made an investigative journey to Winter Park in March of 1884. He liked what he saw, returned to his family in Bloomington and, by July, escorted them to "the promised land". Imagine the pros and cons which went into making this decision! In addition to his wife and daughter, Louise, he was accompanied by a Mr. and Mrs. Charles M. Capen, Mrs. L. W. Capen and a Mr. S.S. Capen. The Capen house (1885), built at a cost of $825 and identified by the half-timbering in its gable, still stands at 520 North Interlachen Ave. (refer to page 81).

* * *

In the years 1880 to 1895 one must have an image of Winter Park, a town never larger than 600 persons, totally surrounded by orange groves. Virtually every family had a stake in citrus - this was the big commercial attraction. Local newspapers proudly proclaimed that there were more than 850 acres of groves in and around Winter Park. Judge John R. Mizell, son of David Mizell, boasted in 1883-84, that his one hundred acre plot from his father's original claim, contained three thousand citrus trees. In a reminiscent letter to J. C. Chase of Orlando, Oliver Chapman, who had moved to Montana, wrote:

We set out thousands of orange trees, mostly on lots on the Boulevard; I have often thought of them and wondered if they survived the frosts."

Indeed, there was a troublesome freeze in January, 1886 which stripped the trees of all their fruit and folliage and chilled the spirit of the grove owners. However, this proved not to be a killing freeze and the trees recovered. Not so, in 1895; the greatest freeze the industry has ever known

Rollins College Campus (1886)

(excepting perhaps those of 1984-85) which decimated the groves with a profound effect upon the economy of the State. Many planters went north; there was no place else for them to go as South Florida had not yet opened up. It was at this time that James S. Capen and a host of others, packed up - headed north - and sought their futures elsewhere. Within a few years Winter Park lost 20% of its population.

THE ORIGINS OF ROLLINS COLLEGE

The founding of Rollins College is entwined and quite concurrent with the founding of Winter Park itself; the same progressive, far-sighted men nurtured and caused each to flourish. This is, when one thinks about it, the usual condition, for Harvard grew with Cambridge, Yale with New Haven, Dartmouth with Hanover, Middlebury and Oberlin with their respective communities in Vermont and Ohio. We cite these particular institutions because they, like Rollins, were the doing of the Congregational Church.

The Rev. E. P. Hooker came to Winter Park from New England in 1884 to assume the pulpit of the newly completed Congregational Church, then located on the site of the present Hooker Memorial Building - behind the Church as we view it today. This church, Gothic in almost every aspect, was of frame construction with the gable end fronting on New England Ave. This principal facade contained a large gothic window. One entered the church through a portal at the base of a tall, square tower topped by an open belfrey and pryamidal spire. Its steep, shingled roof bore an interesting linear design.

Early in 1884 the Rev. Hooker made an eloquent statement, apparently prompted by the suggestion of Mr. Frederick Lyman, in which he embraced the idea of founding a college in central Florida. This idea was again brought before the General Congregational Association, holding its very first meeting in Winter Park, March 1884, in an address by Lucy Cross, a graduate of Oberlin who at the time was principal of an Institute for Young Women in Daytona.

CONGREGATIONAL CHURCH

First Congregational Church (1884-85)

At the next meeting of the Association in January of 1885 the Reverend Hooker once again persuasively promoted the idea in an address entitled "The Mission of Congregationalism in Florida". This prompted the Association to take action; a committee including Dr. Hooker, Mr. Lyman, Dr. F. S. Gale - Missionary Superintendent of Florida -, the Rev. C. M. Bingham of Daytona and R. C. Tremaine of Mount Dora was formed to sound out interest in central Florida communities in underwriting a college. This committee met with the Association in Mount Dora on April 15th where it was disclosed that Jacksonville, Daytona, Interlachen, Orange City, Mount Dora and Winter Park - all were greatly interested. However, when it came to subscribing funds, all but Mount Dora and Winter Park withdrew. Mount Dora's bid of $35,000 was dwarfed by the $114,000 pledged in Winter Park - including a $50,000 gift by Alonzo W. Rollins of Chicago. $50,000 in 1885 would equate to at least $1,000,000 in 1987. The die was cast; the college would be located in Winter Park.

Alonzo W. Rollins was yet another New Englander who went west to seek his fortune. He was born in 1832 in Lebanon Center, Maine. At age 32 he and his brothers built a paper mill which produced print paper. For one reason or another we find him in Chicago a year later where he became engaged in selling dyes and findings to woolen mills as the A. W. Rollins Co. Ten years later, in 1875, his company had capital of $100,000. By the early 1880's, having contracted gastro-enteritis, he commenced to spend his winters in Florida - initially in Palatka. In 1885 he was attracted to Winter Park where shortly he made the munificent gift to the College which has immortalized his memory. Otherwise, not too much is known or written about him. Tragically, Alonzo Rollins passed away in Chicago on the 2nd of September, 1887, little more than two years after the founding of the College.

The Rev. Edward Hooker was chosen to be the first president of the college. Initially, for a matter of weeks, classes were held in the new Congregational church, then on the second floor of one of the few commercial buildings on Park Avenue, until Knowles Hall - a gift of Francis Bangs Knowles - commenced in October of 1885 - was completed early in 1886. Once again, one marvels that a building project of this magnitude could have been completed in less than six months. This first college building was located on ten acres, fronting on Lake Virginia, which had originally been set aside as a hotel site.

Again, as with The Seminole Hotel, a trained builder-architect with some sense of style, was retained to erect Knowles Hall; this man was Geoge D. Rand of Boston. The building was rectangular in plan, of frame construction with a hip roof and lap-siding on the first floor - then shingled to the eaves. An engaged tower, located to the left of the recessed, principal entrance - sheathed from top to bottom with shingle - extended above the roof to a circular, balustraded belvedere capped by a belfry. The interior contained the President's office and classrooms on the first floor, a lecture hall and study room on the second. Shortly thereafter, again with the aid of Francis Knowles, Pinehurst - a girl's dormitory was built immediately south of Knowles, then, in line, a dining hall and Lakeside, a men's dormitory.

Knowles Hall, Rollins First Building (1886)

The faculty during the 1887-88 academic year consisted of the following:

Rev. Edward P. Hooker, D.D...............President
Nathan Barrows, A.M., M.D.Prof. of Mathematics
Rev. L. A. Austin.........................Prof. of Latin
Miss Annie W. Morton...........Teacher of History
Miss L. M. Abbott.................Teacher of French
Mr. J. H. Ford, M.A....................Prof. of Greek
N. Robinson M.A...............Prof. Natural Science
Isabella Diffenderfer.............Teacher of Elocution
Miss Madge Garrett.................Teacher of Music
Miss Alice Guild........................Teacher of Art

"Cloverleaf" (1890), a women's dormitory, was the last building to be erected on campus during the administration of Dr. Hooker; its architect was the son of Prof. Nathan Barrows, instructor in Mathematics. In his unique design, three wings extended outward from a central core - cloverleaf fashion. French influence was evident in its Mansard roofs and the conically-capped, round tower sandwiched between two of the wings. This inspired, compact design allowed for outside rooms throughout. Cloverleaf was originally located on the present site of Carnegie Hall, diametrically opposite Knowles on the "horseshoe". It must have been a very considerable undertaking, in 1908, to move such a large structure to a point west of Knowles II (Knowles I having burned to the ground on December 1, 1909.) Cloverleaf continued to serve as a women's dormitory until razed in 1970 in which year Lakeside Hall, the original men's dormitory, was also demolished leaving Pinehurst Hall the only original building on campus extant today.

Initially, Rollins operated a preparatory school, in addition to the College. The preparatory school was necessary as the level of primary education in central Florida, at the time, left something to be desired. The academic year was divided into three semesters of twelve weeks each. Tuition per semester in the collegiate department was $18.00; board was $28.00 and a room with

Alonzo W. Rollins (1832 - 1887)

Rev. Edward Payson Hooker

Cloverleaf Dormitory (1890)

Knowles and Pinehurst Halls circa 1890.

William Freemont Blackman

light $12.00. The dormitory rooms were arranged in suites of two so that two students could occupy one as a study and the other for sleeping. Students provided their own linen; washing in the college laundry was a matter of pennies. Before the "Dinky Line" between Orlando and Winter Park was completed in 1889, Orlando students walked three miles plus each way, morning and evening. Instruction was, for the most part, by rote recitation.

Following Dr. Hooker's retirement in 1892, and interim presidencies of Prof. John Ford - a charter faculty member - and Charles G. Fairchild, the presidency of the college was assumed by George Morgan Ward in 1895. Ward, again a New Englander, studied for two years at Harvard, then transferred to Dartmouth where he graduated in 1882. Thereafter, he graduated from the Boston University Law School in 1886 and from the Andover Theological Seminary where he was ordained a Congregational minister. He seems to have been uncertain as to the career he wished to follow.

Dr. Ward came to office at an extremely difficult time following the great, legendary freeze of 1895 which devastated the citrus industry. Without prospect of income, many folks returned north; many students could not afford to continue with college. This was one of the most trying times in the history of the State as well as that of the College. Land values became so distressed that when Edward H. Brewer of Cortland, New York came to Winter Park for his health in 1895 he was able to pick-up the extensive groves that Alonzo Rollins had given to the College ten years earlier for a mere $6,500. Brewer ultimately built a home on this property, duplicating his mansion in Cortland, which is still a Winter Park show-place. Another instance attesting to the deflated land values at this time, is seen in that C. Fred Ward, a former mayor of Winter Park, bought a home on fifty acres, with ten acres of groves, for a mere $500!. The most advantageous purchase in these depressed years, was Charles Hosmer Morse's acquistion of the Knowles' holdings for a reported $8,000 - $10,000.

The severe depression which preceded the presidential election of 1896 and the blowing-up of the battleship Maine early in 1898 also posed great problems for Pres. Ward in his endeavors to hold the College together. In this he was greatly assisted by two stalwarts - William O'Neal, who had been elected to the Board of Trustees in 1888 at 24 years of age and the Rev. O.C. Morse who came to Rollins in 1898. O'Neal arrived in Orlando in 1884 where shortly he founded a book and stationery business known as Curtiss and O'Neal. This was, for years, the leading business of this type in the city. In the years which followed he became an officer and stockholder of numerous Orlando financial institutions. He also gave unlimited time to Rollins College, serving for many years as Secretary-Treasurer. His acumen and wide-ranging business connections were critical to the survival of the College. He continued to be an active member of the Board of Trustees for fifty-eight years until his death in 1946.

Rev. Morse, for his part, came from an illustrious family of achievers including an uncle, S.F.B. Morse, artist and inventor of the telegraph. A graduate of Yale he was everything that the word "gentleman" connotes. His background and character enabled him to be extremely effective in fund raising for the College during these difficult years. Dr. Ward resigned as Rollin's president early in 1902 to become pastor of the chapel at Henry Flagler's immense and luxurious Royal Poinciana Hotel in Palm Beach. This would have been a very secure haven after the travail and uncertainties of his Rollins experience.

This brings us to the eventful presidency of William Fremont Blackman whose term in office from 1902 until 1915 was the longest to date at Rollins. Blackman had graduated from Oberlin with a BA degree in 1877; twenty-two years later he earned a PhD degree from Cornell University. When called to Rollins he was Professor of Sociology at Yale. Blackman was an accomplished pianist and his wife, Lucy, a beautiful songstress; conjure to mind the beautiful music they must have made together in Knowles Hall, the Lyman gym or in the parlor of their home - that formerly owned by Frederick Lyman, at the northeast corner of Interlachen Ave. and the Boulevard.

Knowles Hall II (1911)

The Virginia Inn (1912), ultimate successor to the Rogers House

During the Blackman years an endowment fund came into being for the first time, a boat house was erected, the College acquired the Rogers House - the name of which was changed to the Seminole Inn - with the trustees agreeing to invest $10,000 in its improvement. (The larger, original Seminole Hotel, described earlier, burned to the ground in 1902 - the very year of Blackman's appointment. What a tremendous conflagration this huge pile must have made!) With the enlargement of the campus westward, the Cloverleaf dormitory was moved nearer the lake shore to make room for Carnegie Library (1908)-a $20,000 gift from Andrew Carnegie. Sadly, on December 1, 1909, venerable Knowles Hall, which had served the College so well for almost a quarter century, was totally consumed by fire with great loss of equipment - particularly that used in teaching physics and chemistry by the beloved Prof. Thomas Baker whose tenure covered twenty years to 1911 - a period embracing all but four years of the youthful college's existence.

At this critical juncture Andrew Carnegie again came forward with a grant of $25,000 for the rebuilding of Knowles providing an additional $25,000 was raised at large. Frances B. Knowles, daughter of Francis Bangs Knowles whose philanthropy built the original Knowles Hall, then donated $10,000, W. C. Comstock $2,500, and Frederick Lyman $1,000 which, together with other sundry gifts and the insurance from the burned building, satisfied the Carnegie condition. In 1911, exactly twenty-five years after the dedication of the original Knowles Hall, dedicatory services were held for Knowles Hall II.

Once again, the College came up with a very interesting design for Knowles II. It employs a number of the architectural forms which characterize the early, domestic architecture of Frank Lloyd Wright. One sees here echoes of the "Prairie School" style - the descriptive name by which the early designs of Wright and his followers have come to be known. By 1909, when Knowles I was lost, Wright was at a peak in his career; his famous Unity Temple in Oak Park having been completed in 1906. The forms which are so typically Wrightian in Knowles II are: its rectangular geometry, the low pitched roof with broad eaves, the prominent string-course demarcating first and second floors, but particularly the square, banded windows - separated by pilasters - in its forward projecting pavilion, each accented by a sculptured medallion. Similar window treatments are seen in the aforementioned Unity Temple and in the Robert Mueller House (1909-1911) by Wright at Decatur, Illinois - to cite but two examples. The architects, Whitfield & King, who designed Knowles II, certainly appear to have been familiar with Wright's distinctive designs. Knowles II was ultimately demolished in 1984 to make way for the new $5 million Olin Library. (Refer color plate page 17)

Carnegie Hall - the first building wholly given to library use on campus - stylistically resembles the numerous libraries which Andrew Carnegie gave to communities throughout the country. The Palladian entrance is the only distinguishing, stylistic feature in an otherwise prosaic design. Its original, open interior spaces, lined with stacks, have since been partitioned to serve as admissions offices. The architect of Carnegie Hall was, again, the firm of Whitfield and King of New York. By good fortune Mr. Whitfield was a brother of Mrs. Andrew Carnegie.

TWO OUTSTANDING CITIZENS OF WINTER PARK

It is appropriate, at this point, that we turn our attention to two men - one a business man, the other an educator - who in their different ways, greatly influenced the development of Winter Park and Rollins College after the turn of the century. These are: Charles Hosmer Morse and Hamilton Holt. `

CHARLES HOSMER MORSE

Charles Hosmer Morse, like Col. Franklin Fairbanks, was born in St. Johnsbury, Vermont on September 23rd, 1833. He received his education in the public schools and at the St. Johnsbury Academy. At age 17 he apprenticed himself to E. & T. Fairbanks & Company of St. Johnsbury - the nation's largest manufacturers of scales - for the princely sum of $50.00 per year. Obviously he was an achiever, for within a few years the Company sent him to the New York office where, presumably, he was engaged in sales. The year 1858 finds him, at age 25, in Chicago establishing an affiliate, Fairbanks and Greenleaf, of which he became a partner in 1862. Two years later, in Cincinnati, he founded Fairbanks, Morse & Co. which, in a comparatively short period of time, expanded with branch offices in Cleveland, Pittsburgh and Louisville. In 1872, with the retirement of Mr. Greenleaf, the Chicago operation also became known as Fairbanks, Morse & Co. The firm established an immense factory in Beloit, Wisconsin where, among the products manufactured were the following: motors, engines, pumps, windmills, air compressors, feed grinders, warehouse trucks, and letter presses.

Morse first came to Winter Park in 1881, at age 48, in company with his old friend and associate, Franklin Fairbanks. This was, coincidentally, at the very time when Loring Chase and Oliver Chapman were founding the community. Each bought lots fronting on Lake Oceola. Five years later one could buy a lot with a substantial house on it from the Winter Park Co. for as little as $3,000, so Morse's purchase of land was a minor commitment. At this time there was very little to commend Winter Park beyond the climate and the lakes: not the Congregational Church, not the railroad depot, not the Seminole Hotel or the Rogers House, nothing of Rollins College, not any commercial buildings on Park Avenue.

There were in the vicinity, however, some homesteaders tending orange groves - among them, Henry S. Chubb of Montpelier, Vermont who had come in 1880 at the instigation of Franklin Fairbanks to set out a grove on land

Charles Hosmer Morse (1823 - 1921)

subsequently identified as the Eastgate subdivision. Chubb, with his family, originally lived in a log cabin at the corner of what is now Aloma and Phelps Avenues. Prospering, aided by his Puritan work ethic and personality, he subsequently became Mayor of Winter Park (1890) and a Rollins College Trustee. In 1899 Chubb and his wife, Annie, purchased the property and "cottage" bordering the south shore of Lake Maitland where Judge Lewis Lawrence had fifteen years earlier entertained President Chester A. Arthur. This residence still exists at the northeast corner of Park and Summerland Avenues. J. C. Stovin, the English civil engineer, had also established himself in the area in pre-Chapman - Chase days - planting one of the earliest groves in the county in 1875. In 1908, his widow, Mary Stovin, sold their extensive property, which at one time had as many as 2,500 orange trees on it, to the Robert Dhu MacDonalds of New York for $7,500. The "cottage" which the MacDonalds built exists to this day at 161 Palmer Ave.

But to return to Charles Hosmer Morse, surely from 1881-82 onward, he spent many winters with his family in Winter Park. His enjoyment of tarpon fishing must have taken him, via the South Florida RR. to Charlotte Harbor and Boca Grand Pass which still beckon the tarpon fisherman. His deep involvement with Winter Park, however, commenced in 1904 when he added the Francis Knowles estate to his personal land holdings and took over the operation of the Winter Park Co. The transfer of the Knowles property, including hundreds of town lots and considerable outside acreage, was made by a quit-claim deed dated February 13, 1904 for an incredibly modest price, said to have been less than $10,000. This made Charles Hosmer Morse, at age 71, the largest land-holder in Winter Park.

It was Morse who, also in 1904, purchased the Rogers House, Winter Park's earliest hostelry, for $7,000 and gave it to Rollins with the understanding that the trustees invest at least as much in its improvement. It reopened, greatly enlarged with lighting in 12 rooms and ten private baths, as the Seminole Inn. In 1912, R. P. Foley, the manager, purchased the facility from Rollins for $20,000 payable over 15 years. Its name was again changed to Virginia Inn.

In 1905 Morse, who for years had patronized the Rogers House, made Knowles' former residence at 231 Interlachen Avenue - one of the oldest in town - his winter domocile. This he enlarged and completely redecorated in the then stylish Arts and Crafts mode introducing furniture manufactured by Gustav Stickley of Syracuse, New York. This house, named 'Osceola Lodge' by Morse, still exists and is owned by his granddaughter, Jeanette Genius McKean. Morse, greatly interested in citrus culture, owned a number of groves including one in the area now traversed by Genius Drive. He was a member and liberal supporter of the Congregational Church. The City Hall, the golf course, the Woman's Club, Central Park - all are on land donated by Morse.

In 1917 Morse undertook the building of the Morse Block at a cost of $15,000; this was one of Winter Park's earliest brick buildings. Located on Park Avenue north of Welborne, it originally housed Mr. Morse's office, as well as those of H. A. Ward and H. W. Barnum on the ground floor, with apartments above. Quite plain and functional in design - its sole decoration being a string-course under the eaves - it is partially occupied today by The Center Street Gallery.

The Packwood Building, formerly the F. W. Shepherd Building, was Park Avenue's first brick commercial structure. A number of the early frame buildings on Park Ave. were eventually covered with a brick veneer; among these, in 1914, that built by Chapman and Chase in 1882 at the NE corner of Park and the Boulevard. This, the reader will recall, was leased to Ergood and White as a general store. At the same time, a shed-roofed porch which extended to the curb, was removed. The Pioneer Store (1884) at the NE corner of Park Ave. and Welborne was also brick veneered 60 or more years ago.

Morse had married Martha J. Owens on June 30, 1868 while residing in Cincinnati. The Morses had three children: Elizabeth, who ultimately married Dr. Richard M. Genius of Chicago, Charles Hosmer Jr. who succeeded his father as president of Fairbanks-Morse, and Robert Hosmer, also an officer of the Company. Mrs. Morse passed away in 1903. In 1911 Mr. Morse married Helen H. Piffard with whom he lived until his death on May 5, 1921 at the age of eighty-eight. Osceola Lodge became their year-around residence from 1915. (Refer to page 82, also color plate page 35)

On November 20, 1986, in an impressive ceremony attended by his granddaughter, Jeanette Genius McKean, and her husband, Hugh McKean, as well as Mayor Hope Strong, a monument was dedicated in Central Park to the memory of the man and his everlasting impact upon the community; this included a bronze plaque which reads as follows:

"In 1850 Charles Hosmer Morse was an office boy for E & T Fairbanks & Co. of St. Johnsbury, Vermont. His salary of $50.00 per year was not excessive but that was before the Income Tax. By 1871, due to his integrity and skill as manager, he was made Chief Executive Officer of what had become Fairbanks, Morse & Co. Under his leadership the firm produced wind-mills, scales, Diesel engines, and other industrial machines which served this country well in its development of the West.

The instrument deeding this park to the city includes the following: This conveyance being made for the purpose of Parks and it being expressly understood that the use of any of said lands for any other purpose will cause the same to revert to the party of the first part, his heirs or assigns."

"Osceola Lodge" (1882), 231 Interlachen Avenue winter home of Charles Hosmer Morse

HAMILTON HOLT

Hamilton Holt, who assumed the presidency of Rollins College in 1925 at the age of 58, must rank as one of the most dedicated, innovative, humane and civilized leaders ever to have resided in Winter Park. He came to a small, comparatively obscure, parochial college and, in the twenty-four years of his administration to 1949, left by the force of his character and policies, an institution respected as an innovator in the liberal arts. He changed the complexion of the college and, in so doing, enhanced the quality of life in Winter Park. What was the background of this man?

Holt was born in Brooklyn, New York on August 19, 1872. He received his primary education initially at the Woodstock Academy in Connecticut, then at the Columbia Grammar School in New York City. He entered Yale University in 1890 and graduated with an AB degree in 1894. Following graduation he persued graduate studies in Sociology and Economics at Columbia University while assisting his grandfather, editor of a weekly magazine known as **The Independent.** By 1897 he became managing editor of the Independent which in the next fifteen years he converted into one of the most influential periodicals in the country.

A liberal, his life was dedicated to the peace movement, of which he was a prime-mover, and to fair employment practicies. He was instrumental in the founding of the Carnegie Endowment for International Peace. He spoke and wrote widely on the subject of peace. His dedication to this cause won him LL.D's at Ursinus College in 1915, at Wooster College in 1916, at Wilberforce in 1920 and at Oberlin in 1921 . In 1919 he was in Paris at the drafting of the Covenant of The League of Nations as a delegate of the League to Enforce Peace. He toured the United States for four years thereafter urging United States membership in the League. In the meantime he was awarded additional LL. D degrees by Otterbein College, by Baylor and Boston Universities.

In 1924 Holt ran as Democratic candidate for election to the U.S. Senate from Connecticut in a special election and was defeated in this predominantly Republican State. The following July he was offered the presidency of Rollins College at a turning point in his life. Although he had never taught in a classroom or administered any educational institution, he proved to be the quintessential college president. Looking back to his own experience at Yale, he thought there must be a better method than lecture and recitation. In his first year at Rollins he was able to introduce what he called the "Conference Plan" in which most classes met with their professors for two hours every week day during which all work was completed. This was, in some sense, a return to the Socratic method. "Prexy" Holt was held in respectful affection by the students.

Another of his innovations was what he called "Animated Magazine". "Published" once a year in February, it was a "magazine" that came alive. The publisher was Edward Osgood Grover; the editor Hamilton Holt. Contributors read their articles before audiences of from 3,000 to 5,000 persons who sat in the hot, Florida sun to see and hear them. "Animated Magazine" was an event! In this endeavor Holt was able to draw upon his wide acquaintanceships in government, in education and in journalism - including such men as Charles Seymour, Pres. of Yale, Arthur Hays Sulzberger, publisher of The New York Times, commentator Edward R. Murrow, Jane Addams - reformer, Dr. Elbert K. Fretwell, Chief of the Boy Scouts and, in 1935, Cordell Hull, Secretary of State, who spoke on world peace.

Through these lectures the College enjoyed wide attention and an enhanced reputation. Pres. Holt also conceived the idea of the "Walk of Fame", a very interesting feature of the campus, in which the names of hundreds of the world's great are inscribed in stones beside walks around the "horseshoe". Among these is one personally set in place by President Harry S. Truman who was awarded an honorary degree by the College in 1949 - Holt's final year as President.

Surely the most visible, and perhaps the most enduring, of President Holt's innovations is the Spannish Mediterranean architecture which he introduced. Heretofore, as we have seen, the campus architecture, while creditable, followed no particular scheme. Holt felt that the Spannish, or Mediterraneam Revival style, was particularly appropriate amidst Florida's palms and climate. In looking about for a talented exponent of this style he enlisted architect Richard Kiehnel of Miami who designed Rollins Hall in 1930 and the Mayflower and Pugsley dormitories the following year.

When a year or two later the highly regarded Ralph Adams Cram was retained to design the beautiful Knowles Memorial Chapel with funds made available by Frances Knowles Warren, Holt made sure that it was in the Spannish Mediterranean style, so also the adjoining Annie Russell Theatre funded by Mrs, Edward Bok. Of the numerous buildings added to the campus during the Holt administration, all are in this style which has been adhered to now for over fifty-five years and is one of the unique and distinguishing features of the campus.

Hamilton Holt passed away at Woodstock, Conn. (technically Pomfret) on the 26th of April, 1951. The listing of awards given to him in the course of his life - beyond those herein cited - is impressive. The greatness of the man is that, in his first career, he dedicated himself to world peace of which there is no greater cause; in a second career he dedicated himself, with great success, to making Rollins College the premier espouser of the liberal arts in the south.

In his emotional, farewell address to the College, delivered June 2nd, 1949 after having served as President for almost a quarter century, he observed:

> If I had my life to live over again there are not a few things that I would do differently, but I will mention only two. First, I would cultivate my parents more than I did or more than most young people do. After they are gone it is too late. Second, I would try to fulfill in myself at the earliest moment Huxley's definition of an educated man—namely, one who knows everything about something and something about everything. I did not master anything in my life until I was over thirty years of age and I never knew until then the power that comes to one who knows what he is talking about.

He also offered the following axioms:

No college can educate you. All education is self-education.

The college can stimulate, advise and point the way, but the path must be trod by you. *(continued on page 36)*

Above - The William C. Temple Cottage (1878)
Below - Osceola Lodge (1882) Interlachen Avenue

Above - Alabama Hotel (Condominium)
Below - C.W. Ward Cottage, 621 Osceola Avenue (1884)

Get happiness from your contemporaries; get wisdom from your elders. Cultivate, therefore, both your college mates and the faculty.

Major in the courses which you like most and which therefore come easiest. Minor in the courses which you like least and which therefore come hardest.

The human race never has and never will put physical prowess above mental and moral achievement. Do not, therefore, put athletics first.

"I shall miss you, my sons and daughters, in the coming days. I shall miss hearing your happy laughter coming through the open windows of my office. I shall miss the waving of your hands as we pass on the campus. I shall miss the quiet talks I have had in my home with you, whether singly or in groups. Write me sometime and tell me of your trials and triumphs. May the latter far exceed the former".

Two years later, on April 28, 1951, Hamilton Holt passed on from this world.

Hamilton Holt, Rollins President - 1925 to 1949

ADDITIONAL PIONEERS

WILLIAM CHARLES COMSTOCK (1847 - 1924)

William Charles Comstock, the most cultivated of Winter Park's early residents and one of the most enduring since his residency covered four decades from 1883 to 1924, was born in Oswego, N. Y. in 1847. Like Loring Chase, Charles Hosmer Morse and others from the East, Chicago beckoned him. He earned BA and MA degrees from Northwestern University in 1867 and 1870 respectively, also a Phi Beta Kappa degree. He became a wealthy grain merchant and, from 1868-1893, served as president of the Traders Assurance Co, of Chicago. From 1875 to 1924 he was president of the Chicago Board of Trade.

Comstock first came to Osceola, the fore-runner of Winter Park, as early as 1876 at age 29. He became a director of the Winter Park Co. upon its formation in 1885; additionally, he became a charter trustee of Rollins College in that year. He gave liberally to the rebuilding of Knowles Hall in 1910, was one of the organizers of the Winter Park Library and, in 1914, the Winter Park Country Club.

"Eastbank", his winter residence, built in 1883 at what is now identified as 724 Bonita Drive, is one of the most important historic homes in Winter Park. It was so cited by the Winter Park Historic Preservation Awards Committee in 1984. Present-day Bonita Drive was originally a private alley of camphor trees which lead to the Comstock "cottage" then surrounded by a 60 acre orange grove overlooking Lake Osceola. The "cottage" was constructed in the so-called "shingle style" - very much in vogue at the time in the cities of the northeast and at such fashionable resorts as Newport where it was introduced by the leading architect Henry Hobson Richardson and the firm of McKim, Mead and White. Characteristics of the style are: extensive porches, irregular roof-line; curvilinear, engaged corner towers, recessing and/or projection of facade elements and, of course, shingle sheathing. (Refer photo on page 78)

One enters a commodious center hall from a porte cochere on the Bonita Drive facade. The visitor is immediately confronted by an impressive stair-case with stained glass windows at an intermediate landing. The large living-room to the right of the center hall, extending through the width of the house, has a circular alcove at its SE rear corner. Its impressive mantel-piece, one of six in the house, is embellished with pale green tesserae.

A lateral hall, extending to the left of the center hall, gives access, on the Bonita Drive side, to a large dining-room. This features another fine Victorian fireplace and a hand-painted frieze approximately one foot wide which encircles the room - the motif being citrus fruit and foliage. Across the hall Mr. Comstock housed his extensive library in built-in cases which surrounded the sizeable room where, one surmises, he must have spent a great deal of his time. The upper casement windows of this room are still glazed with the original composite of small, leaded, diamond-shaped panes which refract the light most interestingly.

A roomy pantry and kitchen lie beyond the dining room in a portion of an earlier house on the property which Comstock incorporated into his plan when building in 1883. In its earliest days the house was lighted by a carbide generator; water was piped to bath tubs, but flush toilets did not come until later; it was painted yellow with dark green trim. Mr. and Mrs. Comstock were spiritualists; long after Mrs. Comstock's death, her place was continuously set at the dining room table and it was a major faux-pas to disturb it.

W. C. Comstock was a cultivated gentleman. He was a guiding light in a Fortnightly Club whose members read poetry to each other or recounted interesting experiences. High School girls were hired to serve ice-cream and cake following these meetings - among them Jean Shannon with whom the reader will shortly become acquainted. He was a founding member of the Winter Park Library in 1885 which was eventually housed in a delightful, neo-classic, wood, frame building with corner pilasters and a pedimented portico supported by four columns. True to its Greek Revival antecedents, its gabled roof has "returns".

Shortly after William Comstock's death in 1924 'Eastbank' was acquired by the Harris family, including daughter Flora, who graduated from Rollins College with the Class of 1943 and shortly thereafter married John Twatchman, a classmate from Cincinnati, Ohio. (The celebrated American landscape painter, John Henry Twatchman (1853-1902) was a relative). Flora Twatchman has lived in "Eastbank" virtually all of her life.

W. C. COMSTOCK'S COTTAGE.

Comstock Cottage, the living-room

Comstock Cottage, the living-room, alternate aspect

Comstock Cottage, the library

Comstock Cottage, dining-room

Comstock Cottage, the porch

William Charles Comstock (1847 - 1924)

The COMSTOCK HOUSE is one of only two houses in Winter Park on The National Register of Historic Places; the other being the Brewer House - the "Palms"

Comstock Cottage, living-room and entrance hall

DR. MILLER A. HENKEL

Dr. Henkel was born in New Market, Virginia in 1848 of German ancestory. He was one of twelve children, many of whom became doctors. After receiving his medical degree from the University of Pennsylvania, he practiced for approximately twelve years in Winchester, Virginia before coming to Winter Park in 1883. Without question this move was motivated by the debilitating effects of the tuberculosis from which his wife suffered. Winter Park, the reader will recall, was considered to have a very healthful climate. Furthermore, Dr. Henkel had several cousins in Winter Park - among them George Moyers who, even before the arrival of Chapman and Chase, operated a saw mill on the present site of the College.

For many years he was Winter Park's only practicing physician; he conducted himself and his practice in such a manner that he was greatly beloved. In 1886 he built the Henkel Block, a wooden, frame structure at the corner of Park Avenue and New England where it endured until 1952 when replaced by the Barnett Bank. The block contained five, ground-floor units: one of which was originally occupied by a Dr. J. L. B. Eager - a graduate in both pharmacy and medicine - as The Seminole Pharmacy; another by Maxson's Book Store which supplied books used at the Rollins Academy and College; a third unit by Pierce and Mathews Market which boasted "to have always on hand a full supply of all kinds of fresh meat - both northern and southern - also fish, oysters and game, with facilities for handling second to none in the State". A fourth unit was occupied by Capen & Company - general dealers in citrus and real estate. The Henkel Building had twelve window bays across the facade; it was, as were all Winter Park buildings until the twentieth century, of wood construction with bracketed eaves interrupted by a central, decorative, diminutive pediment. A shed-roofed porch supported by simple posts, sheltered the only paved sidewalk in Winter Park. (Refer to photo on page 16)

Dr. Henkel, like almost everybody in those days, was into citrus; he owned a 200 acre grove in Maitland and others in Winter Park. He was a member of the Congregational Church and was either mayor or a councilman during most of the quarter century he lived in Winter Park until his dealth in 1911. He was responsible for the planting of many of the oak trees lining Winter Park's streets. Dr. Henkel and his wife had three children - all of whom graduated from Rollins College are alive today: Thomas is a prominent Winter Park businessman, Fannie, a college professor in Georgia and Anna Maria, a resident of West Virginia.

Dr. Miller A. Henkel (1848 - 1911)

Dr. William Augustus Guild (1827 - 1900+)

DR. WILLIAM AUGUSTUS GUILD

William A. Guild is another of the early pioneers who cannot be ignored in any recitation of the history of Winter Park. He was born near Lowell, Massachusetts in 1827 of parentage with a history of six generations in this country. He attended Harvard Medical School, intending to be a physician, but after completing all the required studies, elected to be a pharmacist - a profession which he practiced for thirty years in Boston.

He commenced coming to Florida winters for his health circa 1880 - first patronizing Palatka and St. Augustine. However having been introduced to Mssrs. Chapman and Chase in 1883, when the latter were busily engaged in promoting Winter Park, he purchased twenty acres on the north shore of Lake Osceola and cleared the land to established a grove. In the autumn he took up permanent residence with his family, consisting of a wife and four daughters, who came down from Boston. One wonders how they made that trip - by boat perhaps to Jacksonville, then for sure, via the St. Johns River to Sanford on Lake Monroe - and what possessions they might have brought with them.

The house which Guild built still exists at 701 Via Bella. A great deal of the lumber for same was hewn from trees felled on the property, however its cypress siding has long since been covered with stucco. The original shipment of paint and hardware, contracted for in Boston, was lost when the steamer "City of Columbus" foundered off the Carolina coast and had to be replaced. From the beginning the Guilds operated their home as a boarding house; it could accommodate 15 guests who enjoyed a commanding view of Lake Osceola from its broad veranda. (Refer to page 80 for additional information on the Guild house.)

The sinking of the "City of Columbus" was the first of several misfortunes to be experienced by Dr. Guild. In the deep frost of 1886 he lost the orange crop from six hundred young trees which were just coming into full production; then he lost the trees themselves in the great freeze of 1894-95. The family subsisted, none-the-less, on what they were able to raise in their vegetable garden.

Dr. Guild, along with Dr. Henkel and others, was active in the planting of shade tress along Winter Park's avenues. His daughter, Clara, graduated with Rollins first class in 1890. She is believed to have been the first recipient of a college degree in the State of Florida. In addition to being an outstanding school teacher, she became assistant to the principal of the public school at a salary of $40.00 per month. Clara was founder of the Rollins College Alumni Association.

Sister Alice organized the Art Department at Rollins College; her name appears on the list of its original faculty members. The celebration of the Guild's Golden Wedding Anniversary in 1899 must have been a notable occasion in Winter Park where, at the turn of the century, the population numbered 636. (Even as recently as 1920 the population of Winter Park was only 1,079; the explosive growth of the community took place between 1940 and 1960 when the population soared from 4,715 to 17,162).

The Guild Cottage (1884)

ALABAMA HOTEL - WILLIAM C. TEMPLE

The Alabama Hotel was built in 1921 overlooking Lake Maitland on Alabama Drive opposite Via Tuscany on property formerly owned by William C. Temple. The Victorian Temple house was moved to one side of the property to make way for it. Temple's life was very involved and comparatively short. He was born in Starke, Florida in 1862 and passed away in 1917 - a life-span of only 55 years. He packed many experiences into those years. After graduating from the Delaware State Normal School in 1879, he went to Milwaukee where he became associated with the meat-packing house of Plankinton and Armour. Shortly, he returned to his native Florida and engaged in the lumber business for a couple of years - then became manager of an orange grove on the St. Johns River. In 1885, at the age of 23, we find him in New York City involved with several electrical enterprises - the leading edge of technology at that time. Then on to Pittsburgh where he became a district manager for Babcock & Wilcox Co. manufacturers of boilers. Obviously very successful in this connection, he ultimately became a director in a score of companies including banks and others engaged in lumber, coal and mining.

Temple first came to Winter Park in 1898 at age 37. In 1904 Carrie Temple, his wife, purchased the property, with its Victorian house, on which the Alabama Hotel was subsequently built. The Temples must then have lived much of each year in Winter Park for be became deeply involved in business and civic affairs, serving for some time both as mayor and as a trustee of Rollins College. In 1909 he was active in forming the Florida Citrus Exchange of which he became General Manager. The famous Temple orange, discovered by Louis A. Hakes in his grove on Palmer Avenue, was named in Temple's honor.

Pres. William F. Blackman of Rollins (1902-1915), who knew Temple intimately, had this to say about him:

Mr. Temple was a remarkable man, of keen, alert and penetrating mind, courageous in initiative and enterprise, independent in opinion and judgement, determined in purpose and inflexible in will, a firm friend and a formidable opponent.

Temple called his Victorian house "Alabama Lodge". A few years after his death in 1917, Mr. Joseph Kronenberger of Cleveland, Ohio, a real estate operator, purchased the property and with some associates formed the Alabama Hotel Company. When completed c.1922 the hotel had eighty rooms on four floors and was, without doubt, the most fashionable place to pass the winter season for a number of years. Mssrs. E. J. LaChance and Henry Schenk first leased the hotel in 1932 and then purchased it in 1936. In 1960 the facility was acquired by Mayell-Alabama of Winter Park, Inc. and in 1979 converted into some 20 odd luxury condominium units. The lovely, more-or-less neo-classical refectory of the Temple House, which served as a kitchen for the hotel, has become the condominium clubhouse. (Refer to frontispiece)

William C. Temple Cottage (c.1878), 1700 Alabama Drive

William C. Temple (1862 - 1917)

HAROLD A. WARD

The Ward family figured prominently in the early history of Winter Park. Harold (H. A.), was born in Burlington, Vermont in 1878 - not far from Montpelier where his father had been born in 1848. The senior Ward (C. H.) came to Orange Park, Florida, near Jacksonville, in 1879, but seven years later, in 1886, moved with his family to Winter Park where he engaged in citrus culture. The Ward family's leased groves were decimated by the great freeze of 1894-95. However, father and son bought several groves thereafter at sacrifice prices and brought them back into production including the former house and grove of Holland A. Griswold on the south shore of Sylvan Lake where the senior Wards lived for many years. (Photo on page 82)

The younger Ward, Harold A., attended Rollins Academy graduating with the Class of 1895. Thereafter, he became associated with the Pioneer Store until, in 1904, he became manager of the Winter Park properties which Charles H. Morse had just acquired from the Knowles estate. In fact, Ward is said to have been instrumental in urging Morse to purchase this property comprising some 1,000 building lots and other lands. He continued in this capacity and as Secretary of the Winter Park Land Co. until Morse's death in 1921. H. A. Ward was, at one time or another, tax collector, tax assessor, city clerk, alderman and mayor of Winter Park as well as an officer in several Winter Park companies and clubs. Additionally, he served as a member of Rollins College Board of Trustees.

In its day a great many people of distinction stayed at the The Alabama. Among these were: Edwin H. Anderson, Director of the New York Public Library; Admiral Richard Henry Leigh, Commander-in-Chief of the U.S. Fleet; General Joseph Baer; Henry Morgenthau, Sr., Ambassador to Turkey; Jacob Gould Schurman, Pres. of Cornell University, Ambassador to China and Turkey; Sinclair Lewis, Dorothy Thompson, Margaret Mitchell, Thomas Watson, George Koussevitsky, and Harlow Shapley, Harvard Astronomer among others.

Golf Club-house (1912-14), corner Interlachen & Webster Avenues

CREALDE SCHOOL OF ART

In 1975 William S. Jenkins founded The Crealde School of Art. This is located adjacent to the Crealde Mall just off Aloma Avenue near Winter Park's eastern city limits. Crealde Arts, Inc. is a non-profit arts organization with two divisions: Crealde School of Art and Art Reach. The Art School serves about 1,500 students annually with daytime and evening classes in painting, sculpture, photography, ceramics, etc.. Beautiful gardens behind the School's classroom buildings, with paths leading to a small lake, create an inspirational ambience for the artist. The School is a great resource for Winter Park as is also the splendid Maitland Art Center with roots going back to 1930 when Andre Smith established an art studio there near Lake Sybelia.

Dr. Ingram House (c. 1937) 842 Laurel Rd. (Orlando)
James Gamble Rogers II, architect
Photo - courtesy Gamble, Lovelock & Fritz

Crealde School of Art, Aloma Avenue

Crealde School of Art, alternate aspect

JAMES GAMBLE ROGERS II, ARCHITECT

Let us now turn our attention to a gifted architect who, as much as any other single individual, shaped the direction of the domestic architecture in Winter Park at a critical time when both the community and the College were expanding.

James Gamble Rogers II was born in Chicago, Illinois in 1900, but spent his boyhood years in the northshore suburbs of Wilmette and Winnetka. His father, an MIT trained architect, moved to Daytona Beach when the young Rogers was fifteen years of age. Following graduation from Daytona High School in 1918, Rogers went to work at a local bank for a few years before entering Dartmouth College in 1921. There he studied with an art instructor who greatly stimulated his interest in, and appreciation of, architecture. Dartmouth had no curriculum in architecture, but in his third year he enterd its Thayer School of Civil Engineering where he could not have studied for more than a year when the failure of his father's health called him back to Daytona: he never graduated. While in college he was a stellar member of the varsity swimming team — winning the New England Intercollegiate breast-stroke championship and an All-American citation.

Rogers, obviously possessed of an innate sense of design, assisted his father summers during the college years and, at his side, imbibed the "nuts and bolts" of the profession for he was able to step into the latter's architectural practice and keep it going - so successfully, in fact, that in 1928 he opened a branch office in Winter Park where, upon his father's death, he established his own practice.

The first home he built was for himself on what has come to be known as the "Isle of Sicily". As early as 1925 developers became interested in this scenic property jutting into Lake Maitland, but the bust following the land boom of the early 1920's brought real estate activity to a stand-still. The Island, low-lying and marshy, provided a very considerable challenge to a surveyor. Rogers, recognizing that it would make a terrific homesite, offered to do the survey and lay out twelve building sites for free, if the developers would give him a one acre lot on which he pledged to build a residence that would "stop the traffic". They agreed; the architect tells the story in his own words:

"I called Bob Orwell, a friend from Daytona Beach who owned a Sikorsky amphibian airplane, and asked him to fly me over the island so that I could photograph it. (With my limited funds a 12 acre survey was out of reach). I laid out a 300 foot baseline in black on the white sand and took sufficient photographs so that I could plot the island within reasonable scale. The result was that the owners deeded me a centrally located lot, 165 feet wide - extending water to water - with a depth of about 160 feet. In the meantime I had contacted the Associated Gas and Electric Co. who had the Winter Park franchise, and got an agreement from them to run electricity one-half mile, more or less, from Maitland Ave. to the island providing that I would buy from them one Kelvinator refrigerator, an electric range and $100 worth of stock....The utilities to the island did not include water, but this was not a problem since we had the lake water tested and the results showed that it was fit to drink. We installed a pressure water system using lake water, but did buy drinking water delivered once a week in five gallon jugs".

Later in the year Rogers brought his bride to the home, "Four Winds", which he built upon it at a total cost of $13,000. It was a charming little place designed in the French Provincial style. Although publicized in seven architectural magazines and one book, it did not do as well for the developers as they had hoped; the second lot was not sold until seven years later! The Rogers lived in this house until 1949 - leaving mainly because he was nervous about daily leaving his wife in what, at the time, was a remote location. In the 1960's this property was sold for $250,000 and is now said to be worth more than $600,000. The architect is unhappy with what he considers to be an insensitive addition recently made to the south end of the home. However, he still regards this modest house as being one of his very best building projects.

An early commission which also received favorable notice was designed in 1930 for the Traylor family in Casselberry, north of Winter Park. While small, the architect spoke endearingly about it to the author. Also in the French Provincial mode, all interior, exposed beams were hand-hewn. Its outstanding feature, in conformity with the style, being an engaged, round tower with a conical cap.

In 1932 Rogers had the opportunity to design the dwelling for which he is perhaps best known, namely the Barbour House, otherwise known as 'Casa Feliz', located on a choice property fronting on both Interlachen Avenue and Lake

"Four Winds" (1929) James Gamble Rogers II Isle of Sicily house

"Four Winds" floor plan

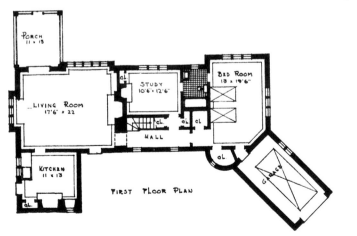

This house with its low-lying roof lines settles down comfortably into the Florida landscape. It is planned to take advantage of a lake on the southwestern side, hence all the main rooms face in this direction. The house is planned for two adults

Osceola. He describes this as being a "typical Andalusian cortijo". What follows is the architect's own story of how it came to be built as related to the author: (refer also to page 90)

Barbour was a chemist. In the course of some western travels one day he witnessed the purchase of a few pounds of a blue powder in a small-town general store. When the customer had departed, he asked the proprietor about the powder and was advised that it was a "blueing" used to whiten clothes following laundering. Barbour purchased a few pounds of it and took it back east for analysis. Before long he had a plant in operation in the Boston area, employing three men, which supplied liquid blueing to the nation; this made him a wealthy man. Barbour, then, in the course of his travels, came upon my Traylor House - actually one of several along similar lines I had designed in Casselberry. Barbour resolved, "That's the man I want to design my house." - and so it was that I received this wonderful opportunity.

Inside and out the house exhibits a remarkable feel for the Spanish Country style both in its design and the selection of materials. One wonders where Rogers acquired such sensitivity to an alien mode, native to a country upon which he had never set foot. The same question might as well be asked of fabled Addison Mizner who, in Palm Beach, during the 1920's and early 1930's, built in much the same style for its many affluent winter rusticators. In Rogers case perhaps the answer lies in the proximity of Spannish St. Augustine to Daytona where the architect had spent his youth and young manhood. Also, of course, Rogers had the opportunity to observe the work of Miami architect Richard Kiehnel whom Hamilton Holt brought to the Rollins campus in 1929-30. Furthermore, he was in a position to have observed the building of the Knowles Memorial Chapel - Annie Russell Theatre complex (1931-32) - projects of the esteemed New York architect Ralph Adams Cram. Actually, Rogers owns to having absorbed a great deal in visitations to Palm Beach and Boca Raton where, in the 1920's, the renowned Addison Mizner was grandly espousing Spannish Renaissance architecture - and to Miami. It is worth noting that there is a similarity in the Florida careers of James Gamble Rogers II and Addison Mizner in that neither completed a formal

"Casa Feliz"- the Barbour House (1932)

"Casa Feliz", courtyard entrance

"Casa Feliz" - the living-room

"Casa Feliz" - the library

"Casa Feliz" - circular, tower stair, entrance hall

education in architecture and that both evidenced a strong preference for, and sensitivity to, the Spannish Renaissance style.

What are the hall-marks of this style as practiced by Rogers? First, is the emphasis given to the gently sloping roof overlaid with half-round, red clay tiles; then the ubiquitous, cantilevered, shed-roofed balconies of wood construction and/or the arcaded loggias and passageways connecting elements. The outer fabric of the house is almost always of stucco in an off-white, buff or other pastel color. Finally, the houses usually have a low profile and tend to be rambling.

In 1936 Rogers designed a stunningly romantic residence in the Spannish style, fronting on Lake Oseola at 1430 Elizabeth Drive, for George Holt - son of Rollin's president, Hamilton Holt. On first encountering this, one even slightly familiar with Rogers' style, feels certain that it must have come from his drawing-board. In the same year he designed a residence on the Isle of Sicily for Mr. and Mrs. Paul Burress now owned by Mr. and Mrs. John Tiedtke - the second, after his own, to be built on the Isle. In the latter he adopted the half-timbered forms of an English country cottage, but this is so rustic in its arboreal setting that one hardly realizes that the architect has momentarily departed from Spannish forms. In 1937 Rogers received a commission to design the McAlester House at 160 Alexander Place - once again employing Spannish idioms.

The following year (1938), the Ingram family approached Rogers wishing to duplicate the house just completed for the McAlesters. He would not do this, however did finally accommodate his client by duplicating the McAlester floor plan, but employing French Provincial forms on the exterior. In a residence designed for Mr. and Mrs. Dolf Keene in Orlando (1937), Rogers forsook the informal country styles (Spannish, English and French) for a stately Georgian Colonial rendition complete with an impressive two story, pedimented portico - thereby demonstrating his versatility when called for by the client. Shortly thereafter he received a major commission to design another Georgian Colonial home on Lake Maitland in Winter Park for Mrs. F. A. Mizener - more on this in a later section.

With the advent of World War II home-building commissions were few and far between. Rogers, Lovelock and Fritz, the firm he founded in 1935, existed on such government sponsored building projects as it could win. Rogers, for his part, was called upon by the U.S. Corps of Engineers to head the Architectural Section of the District Office at Wilmington, North Carolina. Following the war the complexion of the firm changed as it became heavily involved in large institutional commissions including, in 1949, the impressive Florida Supreme Court Building executed in the Roman classic style with a domed rotunda.

Here, the exterior walls are of poured concrete rubbed smooth, its columns of Tennessee verde antique marble. Other major projects were undertaken, in the years which followed, for the Defense Department and the Space Administration. Domestic architecture was no longer a paying proposition for Rogers, Lovelock and Fritz.

Following World War II Roger's firm virtually became the official architects of Rollins College for which it designed a total of at least seven buildings - all adhering to the Spanish Revival style adopted for the campus by Pres. Hamilton Holt. One of the more important of these was the Mills Memorial Library - the Carnegie of 1908 having been outgrown. When built, at the head of the "horseshoe" in 1950, it was believed that Mills would serve the College's needs until the end of the century. Another of the larger commissions undertaken at Rollins was that for the $3.5 million Archibald Granville Bush Science Center in the design of which Hugh McKean, Pres. of the College, former Prof. of Art and artist, must be credited for important contributions. In 1984, in his 84th year, Rogers was called upon, once again, to design the new $4.5 million state-of-the-art Olin Library - the Mills Library having now become inadequate. It occupies the former site of Knowles Hall II, which was demolished to accommodate it.

It is a fateful coincidence that Gamble Rogers II - the nephew of James Gamble Rogers (1867-1947), who introduced the Gothic style to Yale University with the Harkness Quadrangle (1917) and other buildings, should have played such an important role in the development of another campus in an entirely different architectural idiom at Winter Park, Florida. Obviously architecture is in the Rogers blood. Additional residential commissions executed by James Gamble Rogers II will be brought to the reader's attention in a later chapter.

As has been emphasized, Rogers' Spanish Renaissance buildings on campus follow the tradition set with the building of Knowles Memorial Chapel (1931) designed by Ralph Adams Cram, who is best known for his work on the nation's largest cathedral, St. John-the-Devine in New York City - a project on which he worked for thirty-one years between 1911 and 1942. This Chapel is extremely restrained

George Holt House (1936) 1430 Elizabeth Drive

House built for Mrs. Barker (1936), 476 Sylvan Dr.

Archibald Granville Bush Science Center, entrance

Portal, Knowles Memorial Chapel

Knowles Memorial Chapel (1930)

in its design. Its engaged tower was surely inspired by the Giralda Tower beside the great Gothic cathedral in Seville, Spain; one also, however, sees the influence of Sir Christopher Wren in its upper stages. The expansive, undecorated white spaces in the tower's lower stage might have been enlivened by an incised geometric pattern in the Mudejar tradition, but it was not. The architect might also have adopted the florid patterning of the Plateresque on the Chapel's facade, but he did not. But for the half-round tympanum over its principal portal, there is not a curved baroque line, so characteristic of the Spanish Mission churches in the southwest, to accent the Chapel's roof lines.

We do not cite these omissions to denigrate the Rollins chapel which is beautiful in its simplicity, but to point out that it is, indeed, a very distilled rendering of its type - as are all those to follow for which it served as paradign.

Aside from the acroteria and the "Wrenian" tower, the principal decorative element on the chapel's exterior is the finely conceived portal and the marvelous relief sculpture within its tynpanum. This bas-relief, designed by William F. Ross & Co. of Cambridge, Mass. in colaboration with the architect and executed in situ, depicts the planting of the first Christian cross on the continent with Florida Indians looking on at the left and Spannish conquistadors at the right. The Chapel's interior consists of a commodious nave with side aisles. The former is spanned by great masonry arches - employing "Floridene", a native Florida stone - the outward thrust of which is neutralized by exterior butressing. The trussed roof between the stone arches is constructed of treated wood.

All of the many buildings added to the Rollins campus since the 1931 Knowles Memorial Chapel and adjoining Annie Russell theatre, including those from James Gamble Rogers' drawing-board, adhere to this distilled, pristine mode established by Cram: roof slopes are shallow, entrances are arched, profiles are low, covered colonnades are often featured, asymmetry predominates, recessed loggias are introduced and half-round, red tile roofs are the rule.

There are a number of lovely entrances on campus. That on the western facade of Knowles Chapel, which glows in the late afternoon sun, has already been mentioned. The Archibald Granville Bush Science Center has three worthy of note: the first and most obvious of these being its principal portal with a unique, pedimented, scrolled element atop its architrave; then, nearby, the attractive, dual-columned loggia providing admittance to its auditorium; finally, there is a loggia entrance, often unseen and unappreciated, at the rear of the Center's south facade facing the Warren Administration Building.

Across the way a loggia on Roy E. Crummer Hall's west facade is, again, particularly pleasing when illumined by the late afternoon sun. Pugsley Hall, from the atelier of Miami's Richard Kiehnel, dating back to 1930, has perhaps the most convincingly Spannish portal on campus. The many other artistic details introduced into these buildings ought not be overlooked.

Mills Memorial Library (1950), Rollins College

Garden between Knowles Memorial Chapel and Annie Russell Theatre

James Gamble Rogers II, architect

Warren Administration Building, entrance (center)

Pugsley Hall - portal (upper right)

Archibald Granville Bush Science Center (c. 1966)

Above - Scenic Boat Tour Dock - foot of Morse Blvd.
Below - "Emily Fountain", Central Park

Above - Cyclists make a rest stop - Kraft Gardens
Below - Central Park during the annual Art Festival

ROLLINS COLLEGE - THE LATE YEARS

THE HUGH F. MCKEANS; THADDEUS SEYMOUR

We have seen earlier in these transcribings that the Hamilton Holt years at Rollins, from his belated inauguration February 21, 1927 to his last commencement June 2, 1949, were years of great development for the college - in the growth of the faculty, in the adoption of the innovative "Conference Plan" and in additions to the physical plant. They were years of stability fostered by the character of the man who earned the respect of both trustees and faculty as well as the affection of the students.

His was a difficult act to follow as his immediate successor, Paul Wagner, was to learn. Wagner's attempted innovations into the new realm of audio-visual teaching techniques (he had been a Bell & Howell executive) ran counter to the direct teacher-student dialogues introduced by Holt. His early, perfunctory dismissal of nineteen faculty members as an economy measure, albeit with the consensus of the trustees, produced a state of pandemonium on campus for several months which lead the trustees to request his resignation.

Wagner was succeeded by Hugh F. McKean, a Rollins graduate with the Class of 1930 and an Instructor in Art on the faculty since 1932. Having entered Rollins at the inception of Hamilton Holt's regime, McKean was steeped in the latter's modus operandi and innovations, most of which he retained - including the popular "Animated Magazine". His bearing and confident demeanor together with his academic qualifications, instilled confidence and loyalty on the part of the faculty; sanity and calm soon returned to the distraught campus. To assist McKean, the trustees appointed Alfred J. Hanna, a former Holt aide, as First Vice President; John Tiedtke, a long-time trustee, was named Vice President and Treasurer.

The McKean administration (1952-1969) embraced years of significant growth and development at Rollins: the number of PhDs on the faculty was doubled, the student body doubled, the endowment quadrupled, a Center for Practical Politics was instituted, a dynamic interdisciplinary curriculum introduced. Additionally, such important buildings as the Archibald Granville Bush Science Center, the Enyart-Alumni Field House, Crummer Hall (for the School of Business Administration) and the College Art Center were conceived and/or realized during McKean's presidency and 5-year chancellorship that followed thereafter.

Hugh McKean was born on the 28th of July in 1908 at Beaver Falls, Pennsylvania. After graduation from Rollins he attended Williams College, home of the outstanding, collegiate, Sterling and Francine Clark Gallery where, in 1932, he earned a Master of Arts degree. That autumn he commenced teaching art at Rollins - a career that was interrupted between 1942 and 1945 when, during World War II, he ultimately became a Lieut. Commander in the United States Naval Reserve attached to the Advanced Naval Intelligence School.

Returning to Winter Park at the conclusion of hostilities in 1945, McKean married Jeannette Genius, daughter of Dr. Richard Genius of Chicago and Winter Park, granddaughter of Charles Hosmer Morse whose career we have chronicled earlier. The newly-weds moved directly into Osceola Lodge, 231 Interlachen Avenue, which as has been mentioned, Jeannette's grandfather had redecorated in the then avant-garde Arts and Crafts mode with furniture from the highly regarded Gustav Stickley workshop. This must have been a delight to the young couple, both steeped in art and design, who would have appreciated this period decor well in advance of the present-day re-evaluation and re-acceptance of it.

In the autumn of 1930, following graduation from Rollins, Hugh McKean was awarded a fellowship to study at Laurelton Hall, the home and studio of Louis Comfort Tiffany (1848-1943), located at Oyster Bay, Long Island, N.Y.. Tiffany, the son of Charles Louis Tiffany, founder of New York's famous jewelry emporium, resisted entering his father's well-established business in order that he might follow his own artistic bents which lead, ultimately to the experimentation with art glass for which he is best known. He became, in the 1890's, one of the nation's most highly regarded designers and fabricators of stained glass windows and other objects d'art in glass. Early on, he developed a beautiful iridescent, metallic glass which he named "Favrille".

Tiffany windows were very much in demand as memorials in churches so that today they may be seen in virtually every major eastern city. Tiffany lamps, glass shades, candlesticks, compotes, vases and containers of every description are highly priced by collectors who pay enormous prices for them. There are those, including this author, who feel that virtually everything touched by the hand of Louis C. Tiffany is a thing of beauty.

Hugh McKean's first-hand exposure to Tiffany, his works and extraordinarily beautiful home were to play an important role in his career for he and his wife, Jeannette Genius McKean, were to become foremost collectors of Tiffany art. His book, "The Lost Treasures of Louis Comfort Tiffany" (Doubleday, 1980) is the definitive work on the subject.

Initially, the McKean collection was exhibited at the College's Morse Gallery of Art (since renamed the Harriet W. and George D. Cornell Fine Arts Center). However, in recent years it has been on view at the privately owned Morse Gallery of Art located at 133 East Welborne Avenue in Winter Park. This passion for the art of L. C. Tiffany has been a major interest of the McKeans for longer than he had been president of Rollins. The McKeans are today, perhaps, as well known for their collection and expertise in this field as for their long association with the College - dear though this is.

Annie Russell Theatre (1931)

Hugh F. McKean, President of Rollins College (1952 - 1969)

JEANNETTE GENIUS McKEAN, was born in Chicago into a home decorated quite coincidentally, in part, with Tiffany art. With the benefit of hindsight, it is fair to conclude that she inherited her artistic talents from her mother who loved to paint. Jeannette received her education at Dana Hall and at Pine Manor Junior College - both located, at the time, in Wellesley, Massachusetts. Obviously her major interest was art for, following graduation, she first attended the Grand Central Art School in New York and then the prestigious Art Students League where she studied with Helen Stotesbury and Revington Arthur.

Jeannette Genius' ties to Winter Park were very strong even from childhood. In 1936 her father, Dr. Richard Genius, built a lovely home in the Spanish Renaissance style on the shore of Lake Virginia directly opposite Rollins College. This residence, designed by the respected Orlando architect, Morris E. Kressly, is somewhat isolated from public view by a sizeable acreage still in citrus production - part of the original holdings of Charles Hosmer Morse. It is approached only by means of Genius Drive. For many years the McKeans have opened this scenic drive, populated by a bevy of beautiful peacocks, to the public on Sunday afternoons.

Upon the death of her father, in September, 1941, Jeannette Genius inherited this estate and became President of The Winter Park Land Company; she also shortly became a Rollins Trustee - an office in which she served for many years.

Through the years Jeannette McKean has been deeply involved with the community of Winter Park and with Rollins College. Still, she has found time to paint and, with her husband, to found and operate several businesses which help to make Winter Park the interesting, cultivated community that it is. One of these endeavors is the Center Street Gallery where the work of many artists, including her own, are featured. The lovely La Belle Verriere Restaurant, featuring French cuisine and authentic Tiffany windows in its decor, is another involvement of the McKeans. They also operate The Morse Gallery where their collection of Tiffany and other art is displayed with, from time to time, added exhibitions.

A member of A.I.D. (American Institute of Designers), it has fallen to Jeannette McKean to oversee the decoration of a number of Rollins Buildings including, among others, Elizabeth Hall, a woman's dormitory named for her mother. Her paintings are in the collections of The Georgia Museum of Art at the University of Georgia, the Columbus Museum of Arts and Crafts at Columbus, Georgia, and have been acquired by The First National Bank of Winter Park, Winter Park's City Hall and the University Club of Orlando. Her entry in the summer 1953 show at the Butler Gallery of American Art, Youngstown, Ohio, won first prize; Edward Hopper was judge. She was awarded the Cervantes Medal of the Hispanic Institute of Florida in 1952, the Algernon Sidney Sullivan Medallion in 1954 and an Honorary Doctor of Fine Arts by Rollins College in 1962. The McKeans reside at "Windsong" - the home built on Genius Drive by her father a half century ago.

On Thursday, November 20, 1986 Jeannette McKean was the guest of honor at a ceremony in Central Park attended by several hundred of her fellow citizens gathered to dedicate a large bronze plaque honoring her grandfather, Charles Hosmer Morse, who passed away sixty-five years earlier but whose benefactions and foresight have been so important in the development of Winter Park as we know it today. This was surely a proud and gratifying occasion for her.

The Morse Gallery of Art

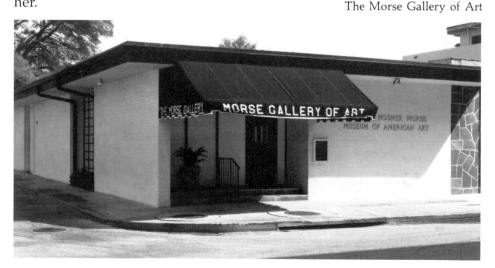

THE MORSE GALLERY OF ART

The Morse Gallery, consisting of over 4,000 works of art, is a comparatively unique entity in that it reflects the combined tastes of a husband and wife partnership - the former an art historian, artist and educator, the latter an artist-interior designer. In addition to the artistic elements obtained directly from the Laurelton Hall, Tiffany's Long Island estate, following its destruction by fire in the mid-1950's, glass objects by Emile Galle, John LaFarge, Rene' Lalique and a glass window typical of those designed by architect Frank Lloyd Wright are displayed. One room is given entirely to paintings including works by such well known artists as George Inness, Maxfield Parrish, Thomas Doughty, and L.C. Tiffany.

A feature of the Gallery is an enclosed, period parlor with rotating decor arranged by Mrs. McKean. At one time the parlor might depict, by means of the artifacts and apparel selected, a couple about to depart for the opera; at another time, an entirely different theme introducing other furnishings and art from the collection. Hugh McKean, for his part, contributes an interpretive commentary suggesting what the set represents. In fact, all of the written commentary and captions throughout the gallery are by McKean. Docents are always on hand to enrich one's visitation of The Morse Gallery of Art - a great Winter Park asset.

Dedication - Charles Hosmer Morse Memorial, November 1986

"Windsong" viewed from Genius Drive

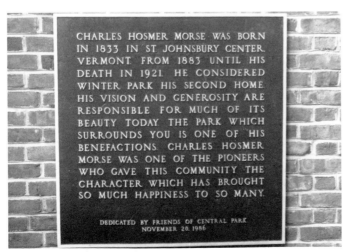

CHARLES HOSMER MORSE WAS BORN IN 1833 IN ST. JOHNSBURY CENTER, VERMONT. FROM 1883 UNTIL HIS DEATH IN 1921 HE CONSIDERED WINTER PARK HIS SECOND HOME. HIS VISION AND GENEROSITY ARE RESPONSIBLE FOR MUCH OF ITS BEAUTY TODAY. THE PARK WHICH SURROUNDS YOU IS ONE OF HIS BENEFACTIONS. CHARLES HOSMER MORSE WAS ONE OF THE PIONEERS WHO GAVE THIS COMMUNITY THE CHARACTER WHICH HAS BROUGHT SO MUCH HAPPINESS TO SO MANY.

DEDICATED BY FRIENDS OF CENTRAL PARK
NOVEMBER 20, 1986

THADDEUS SEYMOUR, EDUCATOR

Hugh McKean was succeeded as President of Rollins by Jack B. Critchfield in 1969, however McKean continued to serve in the capacity of Chancellor of the College for five additional years. Critchfield, a youthful 36 years of age upon coming to Rollins, held M.A. and Ed.D degrees from the University of Pittsburgh where he was in Administration at the time of his appointment. Surprisingly, after eight years, Critchfield forsook the field of education in 1978 when he resigned to accept the presidency of the Winter Park Telephone Company.

A year-long search on the part of the Trustees lead to the appointment of Thaddeus Seymour as President in 1978. Seymour, a scholar, did his undergraduate work at Princeton and the University of California - graduating from the latter in 1950. He earned a Doctorate in English Literature from the University of North Carolina in 1955. With these credentials he became, first Instructor, then Professor of English Literature at Dartmouth College from 1954 to 1969, and Dean of the College for his final ten years of tenure there.

Prior to accepting Rollins bid, Seymour had served for approximately ten years as President of Wabash College in Indiana. Thus, for the first time in half a century, with the appointment of Seymour, Rollins has as its top executive officer, both a scholar and an experienced administrator. It fell to him, in 1985, to preside over the festivities associated with the centennial of Rollins founding and the dedication of a great, new library facility - the state-of-the-art Olin Library. Standing before a bonfire on Holt Ave., opposite the Horseshoe, at the inception of the centennial celebration in April of '85, he related to the assembled students the events which lead to the College's origin; how Alonzo Rollins pledge of $50,000 assured its location in Winter Park.

Thaddeus Seymour is a large, open, approachable man - made to order to lead Rollins into its second century. He is by-way-of transforming Rollins into an extension of the Ivy League in the south. It would not be in the least surprising if his tenure at Rollins equals or exceeds the long, memorable regime of Hamilton Holt.

Thaddeus Seymour, Rollins President (1978 -)

JOHN TIEDTKE

John Tiedtke has been a pillar of support both for Rollins College and Winter Park. He saved Rollins from financial disaster during the Holt administration in January, 1948 when the College was confronted with the need to pay the operating expenses of the college for the next six months, having no funds or credit. In those days, Mr. Tiedtke relates, the entire year's tuition was paid in the autumn at the commencement of the collegiate year. By January these funds had been exhausted; there was the spectre of lay-offs of maintenance and other personnel - payless paydays and defections by the faculty.

At this critical juncture Tiedtke, only recently named Treasurer and Business Manager of the College, took the initiative in visiting New York City in company with the aging Hamilton Holt and there was able to raise $125,000 from a handful of loyal Rollins alumni, including dependable Frances Knowles Warren who contributed $25,000. With this "kitty" in hand and an updated budget for the College, upon returning to Winter Park he approached the Connecticut Mutual Insurance Company for a $500,000 line of credit (bond). There being nothing further that he could do at the moment, he and Mrs. Tiedtke went off to Jamaica for two weeks. Upon returning to Winter Park, he was delighted to learn that the insurance company had agreed to issue the bond; the College was out of its bind!

Over the years, in addition to many other benefactions, Tiedtke played a major role in resurrecting the Florida Symphony Orchestra, formerly the Winter Park Symphony Orchestra, and has served as director of same. He has been a principal supporter and President of the Bach Festival Society of Winter Park. He gave Rollins College its tennis courts.

John Tiedtke was born in Toledo, Ohio where his family operated Tiedtke's, a large department store. After graduation from the Culver Military Academy, he entered Dartmouth College in 1926 with the Class of 1930. He received a graduate degree in Business Administration from Dartmouth's Tuck School in 1931, then, in 1936, became an Instructor at Rollins, and in 1948, a Professor of Business Administration. Also, in 1948, he was named Treasurer and Business Manager of the College. We have seen that at the inception of Hugh McKean's administration he was elevated to the position of Vice President and Treasurer.

Insight into John Tiedtke's business acumen may be gleaned from the way in which he became importantly involved in Florida's sugar cane industry. In the 1920's his family had invested substantially during the Florida real estate boom by purchasing bonds issued by the State's counties. With the end of this excessive speculation, the collapse of land values and the national depression of the 1930's, Florida suffered a knock-out blow; bonds of her political subdivisions were selling at a fraction of their face value. Bankers and brokers suggested that they be sold before they were totally worthless.

Representing the family's interest, Tiedtke came to Florida - specifically to Clewiston - with the idea of converting the bonds to equities. Astutely, however, he observed that while the sugar companies were not making money, they were the only ones paying their taxes. He studied the sugar industry in company with an attorney acquaintance who operated a small "plantation." Rather than sell the family's depreciated bonds, he decided to purchase land in the area which was selling at very greatly depressed prices. This he acquired by paying the back taxes with the family's bonds - worth only ten cents on the dollar in the market, but one hundred cents on the dollar in payment of taxes. In this way he acquired a very considerable acreage, in company with his attorney friend, which they consolidated into what became the "Shawnee Farms" sugar plantation.

These astute and timely investments, consummated in the mid-nineteen thirties, have paid-off handsomely over the years, and have been at least partially responsible for enabling John Tiedtke to be the positive force that he has been for the betterment of Winter Park and Rollins College.

Photograph of John Tiedtke on page 64

Courtyard entrance to Polasek studio

"Evoking Memories" by Albin Polasek

ALBIN POLASEK, Sculptor (1879 - 1965)

There have been - and continue to be - in Winter Park, a great many people, often retirees, who have made outstanding achievements in their chosen careers as the Directory of The University Club of Winter Park suggests; people, who in their retirement, would not wish to isolate themselves from the cultural opportunities available in Winter Park, Maitland and Orlando. Albin Polasek was such a person.

Allow me to relate how I first became aware of him. Early in my explorations of Winter Park as my wife and I were driving on Osceola Ave. en route to "do" Genius Drive on a Sunday afternoon, my attention was drawn to a rather large, white, rectangular, relief sculpture forming part of a low wall before what appeared to be an impressive estate. As the recent author of a book entitled "Outdoor Sculpture in Ohio", I turned to my wife and said, "We've got to look into that on our return"—and return we did, noting a sign in the adjacent driveway welcoming visitors to the residence on Sunday afternoons. We pulled into the drive, parked and while walking to the courtyard preceding the entrance, observed a sculpture to which I immediately related. "That's 'Saint Francis and the Wolf' by Ruth Sherwood", I blurted to my wife, "don't you remember seeing it near the entrance to the Hall of Philosophy at Chautauqua, New York?" What would it be doing here in Winter Park? Observing the additional sculptures within the courtyard, it became apparent to us that this was either the atelier of a sculptor, or perhaps the residence of a wealthy collector.

Within the entrance we were greeted by two ladies - one of them elderly. I immediately inquired as to how the sculpture by Ruth Sherwood came to be on the property.

"Didn't you know", the elder lady responded, "Ruth Sherwood was the wife of Albin Polasek."

It seems that in 1914 when Polasek was head of the sculpture department at the Chicago Institute of Art - a position which he held for some thirty years - Ruth Sherwood studied under him and came secretly to adore him. Nothing, however, came of this unrequited infatuation, and each went about their lives. Polasek had long harbored the dream of returning to his native town, Frenstat, in Moravia and there building a home and studio according to plans which he had for years been formulating in his mind. The Hitler regime, the seizure of the Sudentenland and the rape of Czeckoslovakia brought his dream to an abrupt end.

Throughout his life Polasek had the fortunate quality of making friends with whom he seemed never to lose contact. In 1950, at age 71, he came to Winter Park to visit Ruth Sherwood who had taken up residence here. He liked what he saw, purchased a piece of land fronting on Lake Osceola, and commenced to build a studio-home according to his own design. In December of that year the couple were married - both for the first time. For Ruth this was certainly a dream come true after thirty-six years. Tragically, the marriage was not to last very long for, before a year had passed, Ruth Sherwood succombed in the course of an operation for what proved to be a cancer of the throat.

At this unfortunate but timely juncture, Dr. William Kubat and his wife, Emily, entered the picture. Thirty years earlier Emily had been a contributor to a Bohemian newspaper in Chicago. Albin Polasek had been a reader of this paper and, on one or more occasions, had responded to her articles. The Kubats, too, by a fortuitous chance, had settled in Winter Park and now became fast friends with the sculptor who, by this time, was confined to a wheel-chair resulting from a stroke which left him partially paralyzed. Emily cooked Bohemian dishes for him and helped him in his sculpting. Within a year following Dr. Kubat's death in 1960, Emily and Albin were married. Emily, quite beautiful even at age 80, was the elder of the two ladies who greeted my wife and me upon entering the Polasek residence!

Albin Polasek came to America in 1901 at age 21; he was then an experienced wood-carver. Within a couple of years he had earned enough money to enroll in the prestigious Pennsylvania Academy of Fine Arts at Philadelphia. There he studied under the noted sculptor, Charles Grafly, a master of allegory. While a student Palasek received considerable notice and won important prizes for his work. In 1910 he was awarded a Fellowship to study at the American Academy in Rome and it was there that he

"Lisa and the Swan" - Albin Polasek

Relief Sculpture by Ruth Sherwood - Polasek Studio

"Man Carving his Own Destiny" - Albin Polasek

"Forest Idyll" - Albin Polasek"

"Knocking at the Door" - Albin Polasek

executed the bas-relief entitled "Evoking Memories" - a copy of which inserted in the low wall before his estate - is what drew us to know of Albin Polasek in the first instance.

Over the years Polasek sculpted many impressive pieces; a self-portrait bust executed while he studied at the Pennsylvania Academy reveals a most attractive young man. Sculptress Anna Hyatt Huntington purchased copies of his lovely "Forest Idyll" and "Man Carving His Own Destiny" for display at Brookgreen Gardens at Merrills Inlet, South Carolina. An additional cast of the former, portraying a beautiful, young woman with a new- born fawn in her embrace, reaching for its mother, is located at the entrance to the Winter Park City Hall (would that it were out on a lawn somewhere).

His portrait busts are noteworthy: one of the artist Francis D. Millet is in the collection of the Pennsylvania Academy; his bust of "Daniel Boone", in the Hall of Fame, is one of perhaps only two of his works in New York City. A fine bust of J. Pierpont Morgan, originally displayed at the Morgan Library, is now in Rome, Italy.

Immediately before World War II Polasek executed a particularly impressive monument to the memory of Woodrow Wilson. The American President and founder of the League of Nations was portrayed attired in a long frock-coat, overlaid with the beautifully executed folds of a cape, standing before a chair-of-state. This splendid, life-size image, installed on a high plinth before the Wilson Station in Prague, was destroyed by the Germans in the course of

World War II. What a disappointment this loss must have been to Polasek! Another major commission was the life-size rendition of Father Pierre Gibault, dedicated in 1936, which stands before the venerable Catholic Church dating to the period of French dominion at Vincennes, Indiana - all part of the George Rogers Clark Memorial there.

We have only touched upon the many works executed by Albin Polasek in the course of his long and active career. A fuller exposition and visualization is contained in a fine book entitled *"Carving His Own Destiny: The Story of Albin Polasek"* by Ruth Sherwood in which she, incidentally, shows herself to be a fine writer and chronicler as well as a sculptress. It is well that she undertook this book, as a labor of love, for Albin Polasek had a great talent which is little noted or documented elsewhere - even in such a compendium as *"200 Years of American Sculpture"* published in 1976 by The Whitney Museum of American Art. Certainly there must be many evidences of his distinguished career in and around Chicago where he worked and made his home for so many years. The Albin Polasek Foundation was created in Winter Park to preserve the studio-home which he built as a memorial-museum where his works may be viewed. It is another of the institutions which make Winter Park an interesting place in which to live.

"Emily" by Albin Polasek, in entrance courtyard

Albin Polasek, sculptor (1879 - 1965)

Annie Russell House (1926), 1420 Via Tuscany

John M. Tiedtke, Economist, Trustee of Rollins College

ADDITIONAL WINTER PARK PERSONALITIES

ANNIE RUSSELL

Annie Russell is part of the folklore of Winter Park. The Annie Russell Theatre, connected by an arcaded breezeway to Knowles Memorial Chapel, together form the center-piece of the Rollins College campus. Annie Russell's residence at 1420 Via Tuscany is one of the more important points of general interest in the driving tour of Historic Winter Park prepared by the Junior League of Orlando-Winter Park. Who was this lady?

Annie Russell was an English-born actress whose career spanned the years from 1877, when she was seven years old, to 1917 when she retired from the stage at age 47. Considered to be one of the most versatile and brilliant actresses on the English-speaking stage, she was the first of the so-called "stars" to be designated by theatrical producer Charles Frohman who introduced the "star" concept to the American theatre. Mrs. Edward Bok, whose husband, longtime editor of The Ladies Home Journal (1889 - 1919), financed the construction of the famous "Singing Tower" at Lake Wales, Florida, was a lifelong admirer and friend of Annie Russell. It was she who gave the theatre in the latter's name to Rollins College circa 1931. Thereafter, Miss Russell became artistic director of the theatre and a consultant in dramatic arts at the College from 1931 until her death in 1936. At the 1932 commencement Pres. Hamilton Holt honored her with a Doctor of Humanities degree. Annie Russell's eye-sight failed in her final years. Dorothy Shepherd Smith, a 1933 alumnus of the College, recalls that her first job, while still a student, was reading the Life of Sarah Bernhart to her for 25 cents per hour.

In 1929 Annie Russell purchased the Spannish Mediterranean residence at 1420 Via Tuscany either from Judge Leonard J. Hackney who built it in 1926 or his son, Robert B. Hackney. It has beautiful gardens which have been improved and developed by each subsequent owner. These included Oliver K. Eaton, an outstanding Pittsburgh trial lawyer and one-time mayor of Winter Park, who purchased the house in 1946; then Sarah and Sidney Ward who acquired it from the Eatons in 1960. The art-oriented Wards (Mr. Ward was an art instructor at Rollins) collected Japanese prints and introduced a Japanese garden. During her residency Annie Russell retained architect James Gamble Rogers II to design a Spring Room addition to the house with an adjacent, outdoor fountain which she subsequently gave or willed to Andre Smith, founder of what has become the Maitland Art Center.

THE TROVILLION FAMILY

The Trovillion family has played a significant role in the life and development of Winter Park for almost eighty years. Dr. Jerry Allen Trovillion, patriarch of the Winter Park Trovillions came to Winter Park, along with his wife in 1908 when the town had approximately 575 citizens. In November of that year he established a pharmacy in the now venerable frame building at the NE corner of Park Avenue and Morse Blvd. which ultimately became the very popular Taylor Pharmacy. Here he installed Winter Park's first soda fountain which made it a rendezvous for children of all ages. At that time the roof of the building which extended to the curb, sheltered a second floor balcony embellished with arcaded fretwork; this was supported by three stone columns at curb-side. It ought again be emphasized that even as late as 1912 Park Avenue was unpaved and vehicular traffic was preponderantly by horse-drawn carriages.

In addition to the pharmacy Dr. Trovillion also maintained a medical practice which he serviced with the aid of a 1909 2-cylinder Reo with chain drive. Prospering in these endeavors, by 1910 Trovillion was able to buy the frame home on the sizeable property at the NW corner of Interlachen and Welborne which became known variously as "Trovillion's Grove" or as "Oneonta Lodge". Among other activities Dr. Trovillion was a founding member of the First Baptist Church originally located near the present-day site of Rollins' Crummer Hall.

His son, Ray A. Trovillion, 15 years of age when the family settled in Winter Park, became a beloved figure in the seventy-five active years during which he was a resident. Following three years at the Rollins Academy where he was a member of the baseball team and the college band, he went to work in his father's drug store. In 1916 at age 23 Ray married Martha Perrine who shared his interest in music. She passed away in giving birth to their first son, Thomas A. Trovillion. In that year, Ray became an officer in the Winter Park band which gave concerts in the Park every Sunday afternoon - forerunners of an oft repeated tradition.

In 1922 Ray married Pearl Proctor, an Orlando school teacher, who has survived him and resides in the Cloisters Apartments. Another son, R. Allen Trovillion, and daughters Virginia and Betty Jane were products of this second union. R. Allen, the youngest son, graduated from the University of Florida where his course work prepared him for a career in construction which he has pursued with considerable success in Winter Park. Daughter Virginia (Virginia T. Compton) graduated from Rollins where she was honored with the award of the Sydney Sullivan medallion.

In 1925 the senior Ray Trovillion, in company with three associates, founded the Altapark Realty Company, but apparently disenchanted with the real estate business he became, in 1934, a Special Agent for the Equitable Life Assurance Society, a capacity in which he served for 37 years until he attained the mature age of 78. In these business pursuits he was known by virtually everybody in Winter Park which by 1950 had grown to have a population of 8,216. He became a charter member of the Winter Park Post of the American Legion in 1934, served on the Winter Park School Board between 1935 and 1941 - originally as president - and played trombone in the first Rollins College orchestra.

Having lived in Winter Park for sixty-three years, Ray Trovillion had a long view of the community and its inhabitants which was recorded in a talk given before the Winter Park Historical Association in 1979. This is excerpted in "Tales of Winter Park" published in connection with the celebration of Winter Park's centennial in March of 1982. On the wall of the local history section of the Winter Park Library there is a very interesting and informative map of the town by Trovillion as it existed when he was a teen-ager circa 1910. Ray Trovillion was a popular, respected and

Gazebo beside "Oneonta Lodge"

"Oneonta Lodge", the Trovillion family residence
Lattice work added by Wheelers late 1970s

beloved member of the community. He passed on in December, 1984.

His recollections of the old days in Winter Park, published in The Winter Park Sun-Herald, January 27, 1971, are interesting. He recalled that there were only three autos in Winter Park in 1908 - each had one cylinder; one was owned by W. C. Temple, another by Charles G. Tousey and the third by Dee Batchellor - a merry Oldsmobile. (His father bought the 2-cylinder Reo in 1909). You could not drive faster, he recalled, than 20 MPH, 15 MPH downtown. You had to blow your horn, or be fined, when turning a corner. Bicycles were limited to 8 MPH. It took 45 minutes to drive to Orlando over sand and clay roads - no short cuts. To shop one would take the "Dinky" line at 8:15 AM for 15 cents and return either by the "Dinky" or Atlantic Coast Line. There were only three houses south of Lake Virginia; this area was a thick hammock where fox, coons and wildcat were hunted. The subdivision of this land commenced circa 1921. Trovillion recalled that there were only about fifty pupils in the Winter Park schools in 1908.

A CONVERSATION WITH JEAN SHANNON (1901 -)

It is doubted whether anyone alive, as this goes to press, has a longer or more explicit memory of Winter Park and its inhabitants from the first decade of this century than Jean Shannon, a delightful lady whom providence has endowed with good health and a clear mind at age 86. Her family came to Winter Park in 1903 when she was two years of age. With the exception of a few college years she has lived in Winter Park, without interruption, ever since.

In the 1860's Jean's grandfather, Louis Wallace, operated a grocery store in Towson, Maryland. At some indeterminate point in time following the Civil War, he migrated to Western Pennsylvania where he became a farmer. Jean's mother, Rachael Louise Wallace - one of three sisters - married Bert Wagner; the other sisters were her "Aunt Jean" Webster and Aunt Kate Bradshaw.

According to Jean, Aunt Kate Bradshaw was the go-getter in the family; thumbing through a magazine one day she became aware of Rollins Academy in Winter Park. Her husband was afflicted with serious asthma; baby Jean (her niece) had suffered pneumonia twice before age two and was the only surviving child of Rachael and Bert Wagner. The Bradshaws, too, had a daughter, Louise, about the same age as Jean. The family doctor suggested a warmer climate. "Winter Park is where we're going!", Aunt Kate declared. And so it happened that the Wallace sisters and their brood, including invalided Aunt Jean, came to Winter Park; at first staying only from October through April. Jean's father, a bank examiner, remained in Pittsbugh to "mind-the-store", as it were, and to pay the bills.

Originally, the sisters rented a house known as "the Camphors" on Osceola Ave. near present-day Sutton Place South. In February of the second year the family acquired land on New England Ave. and retained a Mr. Bellows, as contractor, to build a house for them. Located at 433 East New England Ave. this is today known as the Webster-Wagner House. As originally constructed, it contained four bedrooms and a bath upstairs plus one bedroom and bath downstairs for the invalid Aunt and a nurse. (Subsequently, the house was acquired by a bishop who added two extra

rooms on its east side - one a chapel). The sisters and their children lived in this house until Jean's cousin, Louise Bradshaw, married Walter Schultz in a ceremony conducted therein and presided over by Dr. William F. Blackman, Rollins' President.

Schultz's father, owner at this time of the Pioneer Store, corner of Park and Welborne, had three sons of which Walter was the middle one. Two of the sons, Walter and Artie, for some years operated a men's clothing store at the SE corner of Park and Welborne Avenues known as Schultz Brothers Men's Store. Walter is described as having been a wonderful fellow; he ultimately became the second youngest mayor Winter Park ever had. Until his death in 1945 Walter and Louise Schultz lived in the house originially built by Frederick Lyman- on Morse Boulevard opposite the Virginia Inn; this was, the reader will recall, demolished to make way for the Whispering Waters condominium.

Jean Shannon - taken December, 1986

Jean graduated from Rollins Academy in 1919. The family thought that she should be a musician - a concert pianist. She loved music, but did not want to be that serious about it. She took her freshman year at Rollins College where she studied at the music conservatory, then housed in Pinehurst Hall- today the oldest existing building on the campus. The following summer she visited a friend, Katherine Betz, at Oberlin, Ohio and became aware of a kindergarten school there. She had always loved children; that's what she wanted to do! She was, however, engaged to a young man from Oberlin whom she had come to know at Rollins; her family thought it would be improper for her to attend the Oberlin school. Thus rebuffed, she matriculated at the University of Pittsburgh for a year and hated every minute of it; she was lonely in the big city. At this juncture she was finally allowed to attend the Oberlin kindergarten school and loved it; she found Oberlin to be a great deal like Winter Park.

Following graduation Jean taught kindergarten for a year in Warren, Ohio, but disliking the cold winter, came back to Winter Park where she started her own kindergarten in the Hooker Memorial Building then located beside the Congregational Church (the building has since been moved to Hannibal Square). She operated the kindergarten for two years, until in 1926, she married Earl Shannon a member of her class (1920) at Rollins. Earl and Jean, while at Rollins, had gone on picnics together and otherwise fraternized, but they did not "discover" each other until she returned to Winter Park. Following the marriage of cousin Louise, Jean's parents had moved from the New England Avenue house to #173 Stovin Avenue which her father had purchased upon retirement. It was here that she lived while operating the kindergarten until her marriage. Initially employed by the Florida Power Company, Earl Shannon eventually went into real estate.

Jean recalls that when she was a youngster there were no paved streets in Winter Park; all were of sand and clay. The comparatively few sidewalks were made of a coquina bearing cement - dished in the center- or wood. The grade school was in the Eve Proctor section where Jacobson's Store is now located. This was a good, daily walk from the house on New England Ave. for her and cousin Louise.

The Webster-Wagner House (1905)

"Jean, what can you tell me about Ray Greene?", I inquired.

"Well, Ray Greene was a young man from Rhode Island. Dean Enyart, a wonderful man, induced Greene to come to Rollins on a scholarship, circa 1916, to teach gym classes in exchange for tuition. At Rollins he met Wilhelmina "Billie" Freeman from Cincinnati. She was as pretty as she was vivacious. Billie's mother was ambitious for her; she approved of Ray Greene - considered him to be a go-getting, down-to-earth kind of fellow. In 1919 Billie's father, a man of considerable means, bought the lovely residence built by Mr. and Mrs. Harley Gibbs on the choice property fronting on Lake Osceola formerly occupied by the Old Seminole Hotel."

"Billie, having inherited the big house from her father, lived there with Ray for many years. Eventually she sold it, i.e. all but the gate house, which her son now occupies. Ray Greene eventually entered the real estate business; it was he who sold the impressive Brewer mansion - "The Palms"- to

Wagner Cottage, 173 Stovin Avenue - Florida bungalow style

Frederick D. Trismen of Forest Hills, N. Y... Richard Trismen, his son, a prominent attorney in Winter Park, is married to Bonnie Edgerton of Mount Dora. Throughout his life Ray Greene had a special attachment for Rollins College."

"What can you tell me about Peggy Caldwell and Hope Strong?"

"Well, Peggy's father, Halsted W. Caldwell, was quite well-to-do; however, he invested heavily in stocks and bonds all of which he lost in the great depression of the 1930's along with the beautiful house at 916 Palmer Avenue in which the family had lived since 1915. Following this financial set-back he became Manager of the Chamber of Commerce;, Peggy's mother became manager of the cafeteria at the High School. They took up residence in simpler quarters at 155 Stovin Ave. just east of #173 where my family lived. We all admired their resilience in adversity. Notwithstanding these reverses, both Peggy and her brother were able to graduate from Rollins College."

"Following World War II, in which Hope Strong II served as a Naval aviator, Peggy Caldwell taught Spanish in Rollins' newly established School of Continuing Education - mostly to returning veterans. She was a beautiful girl, lovely, most unusual looking. She and Hope were married. Of course, Hope, a loveable fellow, is now Mayor of Winter Park. In 1974 he and Peggy were able to re-acquire the lovely home at 916 Palmer Ave. in which she was brought up. Wodbury and Florence Morris, who had purchased it from her father, had in the interim retained Gamble Rogers to convert its original English Tudor design to a French idiom. Completing the cycle, Peggy and Hope's son, Hope III, an attorney, acquired the other Caldwell house on Stovin Avenue."

"Jean, I encountered the name Ray Rosenfelt; what can you tell me about him?"

"Well, Ray Rosenfelt was a capable and ambitious fellow, somewhat formal in demeanor. Originally cashier at one of our first banks, located across the street from the Henkel Block, he worked his way up to be president. He and his wife, Margaret, lived in the first home beyond the University Club on Park Avenue North; they raised two very nice sons who inherited, or otherwise own, considerable property near the Alabama Hotel. Following the death of his first wife, Rosenfelt remarried and built a lovely home on the former Brewer property - now Trismen Terrace - where he and Sue Rosenfelt lived until he passed away. I really did not know the Rosenfelts very well."

"You bring up the name Tousey?"

"Well, my daughter is a Tousey; the original Mr. Tousey (Charles G.) came from Clinton Corners, New York in the 1880's. He owned a fine house on Interlachen Avenue which was demolished when Gamble Rogers built "Casa Feliz" for Mr. Barbour. My daughter, Betty married his grandson Bill; they had known each other from the time that she was three and he four years of age. Their son, my eldest grandson, is an architect in Chicago. I am, of course, just delighted that my daughter lives here in Winter Park."

Campbell-Strong house, 155 Stovin Avenue

"Who was this Walter Rose of whom you speak?"

"Well, Walter Rose came here from Georgia, I believe; he was smart, likeable and enterprising. Originally, he was the local stationmaster, however he got into real estate towards the end of the Florida land boom of the '20's at which time he bought up all the property now known as Orwin Manor. Subsequently, he bought up the land where Rosemont Country Club is now located - no doubt for a song. He became very rich. He married Stella Smith, one of three daughters whose father, also a banker, owned "Pansy Cottage" on Interlachen Ave. Daughter Berta Smith married Arthur Schultz, brother of Walter who, as you recall, married my cousin, Louise. The other daughter, Louise Smith, married a man by the name of Lettice; they lived in Orwin Manor. Walter Rose died in the mid 1970's. Stella Rose, his wife, now age 97, still lives on Rose Isle; she is as smart as can be and, as you might imagine, not without means."

"Jean, you have lived four-score years and more in Winter Park. What do you think of Winter Park today?"

"Well, it is difficult to get used to the idea that I don't know everybody in town; it has grown so. But I love Winter Park, there's no other place I'd rather be. However, it's a shame what's happening to Park Avenue."

"What is happening to Park Avenue?"

"Well, rents have become so dear that it is becoming difficult for the small, local merchant to exist. I understand that the people who have bought the Taylor Drug Store are paying $8,000 per month towards their bill! Imagine what that building cost! The building at the corner of Park and Welborne, across the street from the old Pioneer Store, recently sold for one and a quarter million dollars."

So endth the discussion with Jean Shannon, an interesting and delightful lady.

"Carlova" (1915) Caldwell-Strong House, 916 Palmer Avenue

Above - The MacCaughey-Taylor House, Via Tuscany
Below - Breneman House - Virginia Drive

Above - Holler-Lewis House, Alberta Drive, Fr. Provincial
Below - Edwards-Carlton House, Alberta Drive

Gibbs-Greene Cottage, 242 Chase Avenue

Ralph E. Hurst House - 863 Interlachen Avenue

DOROTHY LOCKHART SMITH

Dorothy Lockhart came to Winter Park circa 1931 to assist in the dedication of the Annie Russell Theatre for her good friend Annie Russell. She had grown up in the arts in Baltimore and Philadelphia. She planned to stay in Winter Park only long enough to witness the last performance of the theatre's first production and then to return to New York City. However, she did not reckon with the charms of Rhea Marsh Smith, a Rollins History professor whom she met within a few days of her arrival in town. They were married within a year and celebrated 43 years together as recently as 1975.

The Smiths were close friends of the James Gamble Rogers. Rogers designed a modest house for them overlooking Lake Osceola at the southern extremity of Bonita Drive in proximity to "Eastbank" - the Comstock-Harris House. The Rhea Smiths were among those who clustered around Hamilton Holt, Rollins distinguished President. Following military service in Washington during World War II, the Rhea Smiths returned to Winter Park where she initiated the "Town Hall" lecture series which continued for a decade to 1957. Obviously Dorothy Lockhart Smith was one of those vital, involved persons who enlivened the cultural scene in Winter Park. She said of the community:

"It is a city where people enjoy their independence and privacy, but a city that gives you every opportunity. It is not easy to get to know immediately, but nothing that is fine is easy to know - tinsel is easy to see!. It has been very enriching to live in Winter Park. I hope that it never loses its spirit - its heart. Everyone says "Hello" in Winter Park; it has always had the village atmosphere and if it loses that, we lose Winter Park"

GRACE EDWARDS - Edwards House, 461 E. Webster Ave.

This interesting house was built by Benjamin G. Edwards in 1915 on property formerly owned by S. Homer Henkel who operated it as a citrus grove. Edwards died within a year leaving the house to his daughters, Grace and Helen Edwards. Grace had graduated from Wellesley College with the Class of 1894 and earned a degree in Library Science from the University of Illinois in 1898. The sisters developed a beautiful garden on the property which, unfortunately, no longer exists. Grace was, in 1922, a founding member of The Winter Park Garden Club; she also worked towards the beautification of the Rollins College grounds. Additionally, she was active in the Allied Arts Society and the Poetry Society. She resided in the Webster Ave. house until 1938 at which time she built her own home at 425 Alberta Drive where she passed away on New Year's Day, 1945. The City, taking note of her contributions to is beautification and cultural development, set a memorial marker to her memory on the Morse Blvd. divider island. The original Edwards House on Webster Avenue subsequently came into the hands of Dr. William Foster, educator and Rollins Trustee.

Edwards-Carlton House - 425 Alberta Drive

B.G. Edwards House, 461 Webster Avenue

1035 Lakeview Drive (Virginia Heights), 'Bungaloesque'

73

NILS SCHWEIZER; FREDERICK A. HAUCK

It is beyond the scope of this book to consider every distinguished person who has called Winter Park "home" or influenced its development. Architect Nils Schweizer and engineer Frederick A. Hauck are, however, most worthy of mention.

Nils Schweizer was born and raised in Baltimore, Maryland. Following discharge from the Army in 1946, he studied with, or apprenticed himself to, Frank Lloyd Wright - no doubt at Taliesin West in the vicinity of Scottsdale, Arizona. As Wright's southeastern U.S. representative, he spent four years prior to 1956 overseeing the construction of a number of Wright-designed buildings on the Florida Southern University campus at Lakeland, including the innovative Pfeiffer Chapel, the original Roux Library, and the administration building among others.

In 1956, seeing the opportunities for an architect in Florida, he established an office in Orlando. In the 1970's Florida Southern called upon him to design a new and larger Roux library -the original one by Wright having been outgrown. This truly impressive building is so Wrightian in its appearance that one is at first quite convinced that it, too, came from Wright's drawing board. It enjoys a marvelous situation overlooking the other distinguished structures on campus.

To date Nils Schweizer & Associates have designed over 100 buildings in central Florida. Among these is The Orlando Museum of Art at Lock Haven; this 1964 design adapts itself marvelously to the use for which it was commissioned - the display of art and, in its auditorium, the staging of lectures and films on the arts. It is a model which other communities might well emulate. Other major commissions are: the Orlando International Airport, the Orlando Public Library (1985), and the Calvary Assembly of God in Winter Park. By any measure Nils Schweizer is one of Florida's most distinguished architects.

FREDERICK A. HAUCK, too, is a remarkable man. The family is indigenous to Cincinnati where Hauck's grandfather founded the Hauck Brewing Company. The grandfather's fine, brick and stone residence at 812 Dayton Street in Cincinnati is located on what was known as "millionaire's row." Restored, this Victorian house has for some years served as the headquarters of the Miami Purchase Association - the mission of which is recycling funds for the restoration of other architecturally worthy homes in the area.

Frederick A. Hauck was born 92 years ago on December 18, 1895 - and is still going strong. His voice conveys the enthusiasm of a man in the prime of life. Much of his life has been devoted to mining engineering, but through the years he has found time to be very active in civic affairs. In his native Cincinnati he has served as Friend of Cincinnati Parks. In 1978 he contributed a quarter of a million dollars to the University of Florida for the development of a gaseous nuclear core reactor to make nuclear fuels more efficient and is still very much involved in this project. He worked with Albert Einstein during the days of the Manhattan project when the atomic bomb was being developed. For many years Hauck and his first wife spent their winters in a gracious home (second one beyond the bridge) on the Isle of Sicily designed by James Gamble Rogers II.

A Renaissance man, he has honorary degrees in everything from law to literature. Recently in celebrating his 92nd birthday at the Cincinnati Historical Society, in conjunction with the 198th birthday of the city, he said, "I'm going to keep going as long as I can do something for mankind".

Hauck-Bolen House - Isle of Sicily

Frederick A. Hauck Hall, Rollins College

Hauck-Bolen House - pool and dock on Lake Maitland

THE DOMESTIC ARCHITECTURE
OF WINTER PARK

Earlier sections of this work have been concerned with the architecture of Rollins College and the career of architect James Gamble Rogers II who designed many of the buildings at Rollins as well as some of the most distinguished residential architecture in Winter Park. Let us now turn our attention to a general consideration of Winter Park's domestic architecture in the preceding half century, i.e. from 1882 to 1930.

As might be expected, with the passage of time and the development of Winter Park, a number of the larger, more flamboyant Victorian "cottages" have been lost. Among these are the winter homes of Judge J. F. Welborne which was located immediately south of the Rogers House, the John R. Ergood "cottage" near the intersection of Interlachen and Old England Avenues; the Frederick Lyman "cottage", Gustavus R. Alden's "Pansy cottage" which occupied the NE corner of Interlachen and Lyman Avenues, and the Batchelor cottage located on the site now occupied by Sutton Place South.

The high Victorian **Welborne domicile** consisted of a principal, gable-roofed element, surrounded by a shed-roofed porch, with a single lateral wing having a slightly lower roof peak. The juncture point of these elements was accented by an open belfry with a pyramidal cap. The gable ends, in true Victorian fashion, were embellished by innovative fretwork. The combined roofs were perforated by a number of gabled dormers also decorated with scrollwork echoing that at the gable ends. Welborne had, indeed, one of "the neatest cottages" in town; it was completed late in 1883.

Judge Welborne, born in Indiana, studied law in that state and practiced there for several years before coming to Winter Park. At first his law office was located in a second-floor, rear room at the Rogers House and it was there that the Winter Park Hotel Co. charter was framed. As fortune would have it, Mrs. Welborne lived in their new home for only a few weeks when she passed away on the 14th of January, 1884. The cottage was ultimately purchased by W. J. Waddell, who made it his home for a number of years. In

1910 he moved it diagonally across Interlachen Avenue to a lot immediately north of the Congregational Church and operated it as a boarding-house known as the "Osceola House". The Church purchased the property in 1968.

John R. Ergood's Cottage, contemporary with Judge Welbornes, was a notable addition to the Winter Park scene. Its irregularity of plan and massing, its extensive porch and tower element, are characteristics which today would classify it as having been in the "Queen Anne" style - then at the height of its popularity in the northeast. One's attention here is immediately drawn to the engaged square tower which, as it rises through the center of the structure, intersects the roof gable - then terminates in a fenestrated, dome-topped, cupola from which one would have enjoyed a magnificent view of Lake Osceola and the surrounding countryside. Ergood, it will be recalled, in 1882 leased the first commercial building in Winter Park, from Chapman and Chase where he operated a general store. Succeeding Chase, who held the office briefly, Ergood was also Winter Park's original Postmaster.

The large **Batchelor "cottage"**, built in the mid 1880's at Osceola and Ollie Avenues for a reported $7,000 by R.N. Bachellor, a pioneer citrus grower, was quite as picturesque as those considered above. Here a central, two-story facade was appended at one end by an engaged, hexagonal tower terminating in an open belvedere with conical cap; at the opposite extremity this was balanced by a gabled pavilion - both lateral elements being joined at ground level by a shed-roofed porch. It needs emphasizing that these larger "cottages" were executed in up-to-the-minute, contemporary designs popular in homes being built at the time in cities and fashionable resorts in the northeast.

DeHaven Batchelor, R. N.'s son, born at Appleton City, Missouri on April 19, 1874, arrived in Winter Park with his father in 1883; two years later he matriculated at Rollins Academy on the very first day of its history. After completing his education, he opened a bicycle shop on Park Avenue; then, in 1897, married Louise Merryweather. In 1957 the Batchelor house was briefly leased by Rollins as a girl's dormitory.

JUDGE J F WELBORNE'S COTTAGE.

Judge J. F. Welborne Cottage (1883), Interlachen Avenue

JOHN R ERGOOD'S COTTAGE

Ergood-Roe-Tousey Cottage (1887), 656 Interlachen Avenue

Richard N. Batchelor Cottage (1886), replaced by Sutton Place South

Oliver Chapman Cottage (1882), Interlachen north of Canton Avenue

The so-called **"Pansy Cottage"**, located at the northeast corner of Interlachen and Lyman, was built in 1888 by Dr. Gustavus R. Alden for his wife, Grace Alden, author of the Pansy books. It was a large and costly residence built entirely of virgin pine. Open porches, surrounding both ground and second floors, provided distant vistas up Interlachen Avenue.

When purchased by M. M. Smith, a banker, at the turn of the century, the house had no electricity, no plumbing and a wood range in the kitchen. One would like to think that these deficiencies were promptly remedied, but in 1900 such amenities were unusual in Winter Park residences. Plumbers and electricians were unheard of!

Oliver Champan, Loring Chase's partner in the founding of Winter Park, built his cottage in 1882 at what is now #420 N. Interlachen north of Canton Avenue. It had more the appearance of a lodge than the grander, Victorian cottages considered above. Its large, sloping, shingle, roof sheltered a porch which extended around its south and eastern facades affording splendid vistas over Lake Osceola. Our historic photo suggests the random sprinkling of pine trees which originally covered the entire Winter Park area. Chapman's cottage existed on this site until 1938.

Another of the very early cottages to be built in Winter Park was that for the **Rev. C. W. Ward** at 621 Osceola Avenue - a few lots east of the Seminola Hotel. Ward, who presided over the first Episcopal church service in Winter Park held in the Town Hall on April 15, 1883, purchased his lot from Chapman and Chase in March of 1883. His wife Katherine died, unfortunately, in 1884. Ward sold the property to Alonzo Rollins. He then moved to New Jersey where he eventually committed suicide.

Although Rev. Ward's cottage front on Osceola, the more impressive aspect of it may be obtained around the corner on Osceola Court where it is seen framed by two large camphor trees. From this prospective its multi-garbled character is better observed; also its narrow, banded windows (they never exist singly) each containing 10 panes. The Osceola Avenue facade today appears somewhat bare due, no doubt, to the fact that an original porch has been removed. Likewise, the solarium at the SW corner was, without doubt, once an open veranda. An Historic Marker before the cottage notes that in Rollins earliest days it served as a women's dormitory. (Refer Color Plate page 35)

Earlier we described the **Comstock cottage**, "Eastbank", in some detail. It is virtually the only one of the great, early houses of the 1880's to survive (refer pages 37-38). It is basically in the "shingle style" which shares many characteristics with the quite similar "Queen Anne" mode as exemplified by the John Ergood cottage. It is said that in the four years, 1881 to 1885, at which time the Winter Park Company was founded, 63 cottages were built in the fast developing community. Much, if not all the timber for these and many to follow, came from the sawmill of George W. Moyers whose operation was located on a portion of Lake Virginia's shore now occupied by Rollins College. Moyers named Lake Virginia after his state of origin, Lake Sue for his wife, the former Susan Henkel. "Eastbank" is on the National Register of Historic Places.

The **William C. Temple house** (1878), originally owned by the Packwood family, is another significant survivor from earlier times. Located adjacent to the Alabama Hotel, the building of which necessitated its move slightly northeastward, it was approached from Palmer Avenue. "Temple Grove" which, at that time, surrounded the house, occupied much of the land between Alabama Drive and Palmer Avenue east of the Osceola-Maitland Canal. The house has undergone many additions and deletions over the years. It would be suprising if it had not originally been embellished with decorative barge boards and a more intricate porch rail - features characteristic of homes of its period. (Refer color plate page 35)

Upon its acquisition in 1904, Mr. Temple and his wife, Carrie, introduced every convenience money could buy including a private gas plant, a complete sewage system and, when available in 1912, a telephone. Water from a deep well was piped to every one of its five bathrooms. Furthermore, they added the lovely refectory which now serves as a clubhouse for the Alabama condominiums. Upon the opening of the Alabama Hotel (1923-24), the dwelling

"Eastbank" - the Comstock-Harris Cottage (1883)

Geer-van den Berg Cottage (1880's), 155 Brewer Avenue

provided housing for hotel personnel. Considering the house as it exists today, certainly the ground floor, bow-windowed addition with its round-headed windows, is a late, incongruous modification.

The **Geer-van den Berg House** (1880's) is, despite modifications, perhaps the best preserved and most typically Victorian cottage extant in Winter Park, mainly due to the fact that it retains its decorative barge boards and the delicate, stick-style ornamentation atop the porch columns. The appearance of the house and its fidelity to style have been enhanced by the relocation of its entrance to the porch corner. The decorative pediments over the bedroom windows of its lateral wing ought not be overlooked; also, one will note that the parlor windows below are little more than one foot wide. Located at 155 Brewer Avenue, a busy thoroughfare, the house is very difficult to see nestled behind its screen of dense foliage. Dr. Geer, a very early settler, had a cabin at Osceola when Loring Chase first came to the area; he was among those who gave to the fund for the construction of the original railroad station in 1882.

The **Waddell House** at 1331 Aloma was built in 1897 by the William J. Waddells on a 10 acre tract. Its notable architectural features are the delicate archs framing its ground-floor porch and the knob and collar elements in the rooftop gable. The interior is quite plain: the downstairs contains a living room on the right and a dining-room on the left- each with a fireplace; their 9' ceilings make for good ventilation. These is no central hall. The upstairs contains three bedrooms and two baths. The property was subdivided by Carl Galloway who acquired it in 1923.

Henry S. Chubb came to Winter Park in 1880 to lay out a grove for Col Franklin Fairbanks. By 1889 he had prospered sufficiently to purchase the home which still stands at the corner of Park Avenue North and Summerland; this was originally constructed by Judge Lewis H. Lawrence, wealthy shoe manufacturer from Utica, N. Y. and friend of Pres. Chester Arthur. The President visited Lawrence in this house in 1883 - the year of its construction. The principal facade is greatly enhanced by a simple, Federal-style entrance and dual grouping of the porch columns. Like so many of these early cottages, this, too, was surrounded by a ten -acre

Lawrence-Chubb Cottage (1883), 1300 Summerland Avenue

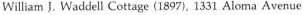

William J. Waddell Cottage (1897), 1331 Aloma Avenue

orange grove which was surely a great source of income until the great freeze of 1895.

When **Dr. William A. Guild**, a Boston pharmacist, retired to Winter Park in 1883, he built a sizeable structure which served both as a home for his family and a boarding-house. Notable elements of its exterior are the wrap-around porch where one may have visions of boarders relaxing on wicker chairs while inhaling the sweet perfume of orange blossoms; also the unusually gentle slope of its gabled roof. This permitted fairly high ceilings on both floors - beneficial for ventilation in the warm and humid Florida climate. It is interesting to compare the historic photograph of this house, standing alone on its considerable acreage which originally extended from Palmer Ave. to Lake Osceola, with our contemporary photo. (Refer to page 41)

When the **Frank E. Spooners** acquired the property in 1905 they converted it into a commodious, single family home and named it "Weatogue" (wigwam place). The house then consisted of 16 rooms including a 40' living -room with a 10' ceiling, exposed beams, oak floors and fireplace. There were six bedrooms and three baths upstairs. When occupied by the Spooners between 1905 and 1925, it was regarded as a "Winter Park show-place".

Although originally approached from Palmer Avenue by means of a circular drive at the center of which there was a rose arbor (for which the house was famous) its present address is #701 Via Bella. While the house is of considerable, local, historic interest, from an architectural point of view, it is stylistically of limited interest.

The **J. C. Capen house** at 500 Interlachen Avenue, built in 1885, provides another "now-and-then" comparison. Originally of frame construction in a vernacular style which harks back to Capen's middle western origins; it was subsequently surfaced with stucco - then anglicized in the process. Note, particularly, the exposed beams in the gable, the changed character of the window below (converted to pseudo - balcony), the introduction of a round-headed window on the ground floor, also the added emphasis given to the front entrance and the conversion of the original, open porch to an enclosed solarium.

William A. Guild House (The Guild Hotel) - 1883

This brings us to the several cottages on Knowles Ave. built in 1886-87 for speculation by **Francis Bangs Knowles**, principal owner of the Winter Park Company, for a cost of somewhere between $3,000 and $3,500. Two of these - now century houses - still survive; one at #232 Knowles and a similar one across the street acquired and recently adapted for use by the architectural firm of Rogers, Lovelock and Fritz. Like a number of others which we will consider, these are in a vernacular style which is to say that they are typical of the place and the time in which they were constructed.

It may be that the Francis Knowles' family occupied #232 for a time, but assuredly, for a few years prior to his death, the family wintered in what we now known as "Osceola Lodge" which Charles Hosmer Morse acquired from the Knowles estate in 1904. The latter was far more spacious and afforded an unobstructed view of Lake Osceola, even as it does to this day. The roof at #232 has been replaced, but its counterpart across the way appears still to have its original, fish-scale, slate surfacing. #232 Knowles, located immediately behind Osceola Lodge, was used during the Morse years as a guest house and has long since come under the ownership of Jeanette Genius McKean, Morse's granddaughter. (Osceola Lodge photo page 33)

Capen-Showalter Cottage (1885) 500 North Interlachen Avenue

Knowles Cottage adapted for use by Rogers, Lovelock & Fritz; built for $3,000 - $3,500 in 1886

Capen-Showalter Cottage as it appears today

Griswold-Ward Cottage, 1401 Grove Terrace

McCallum-Harris Cottage (1887), 1554 Harris Circle

Osceola Lodge, which dates to 1888, was enlarged following its acquisition by Morse. In its present configuration the lodge consists of a center stair-hall with a spacious parlor to its right and a sitting-room to its left. The dining-room, furnished with Stickley-built, Arts and Crafts table, chairs and server, lies behind the sitting-room. The quality of these period furnishings has been somewhat compromised, in the opinion of the author, by the cream-colored paint in which they are finished; Arts and Crafts (Mission style) furniture looks best au naturel.

The far end of the parlor is arranged to form an inglenook with fireplace. Its furnishings are not of Arts and Crafts design, but rather are quite typical of a well furnished interior of the 1950's. It should be remembered that Jeanette and Hugh McKean took up residence here upon their marriage in 1945 and unquestionably the interior reflects her well-disciplined taste. The master bedroom, located upstairs at the rear of the "cottage", is furnished with a painted, curvilinear bedroom set revealing a feminine hand. Servant's quarters are located at the left rear. The cottage is maintained today, one surmises, as a memorial to its distinguished occupant of 80 years ago - Charles Hosmer Morse. It, too, is in the ubiquitous, vernacular style.

Let us now consider two century houses overlooking Lake Sylvan - both located in the settlement once known as Osceola before Winter Park was founded. The first of these, fronting on the lake, is known as the **Griswold-Ward House** (1886-87) after H. A. Griswold who built it and the Charles H. Ward family which resided here for many years. Its verandas, upstairs and down, provide splendid vistas over the lake. In recent years the access porch, away from the lake,. has been rebuilt and enlarged; also contemporary, awning-type windows have been installed. Here again, we have a vernacular design which could have been executed by any good, local builder.

The **McCallum-Harris house** (1887), located nearby at 1554 Harris Circle, consists of rectangular block, parallel to the street, the roof of which is perforated by three wall dormers-the central one predominating. This house is surrounded on three sides by a spacious, shed-roofed veranda; its stylized, roof-top chimney-pots and wall dormers impart a Tudor Gothic flavor - resulting from later modification. Here, once again, a stucco overcoat has been applied to its original wood siding. Even well beyond the turn of this century, these houses and Lake Sylvan were surrounded by orange groves with deep green folliage and colorful fruit.

Oneonta Lodge (1885-86) located at 147 Interlachen Ave., corner of Welborne, is another vernacular design. It is known to have been originally built by Dr. J. E. Brecht, a dentist, on a six acre plot extending to the shore of Lake Osceola. In 1910 it was acquired by Dr. and Mrs. J. A. Trovillion under whose ownership the property became known as "Trovillion Grove" -as has been mentioned earlier. Today, the character of the original house is barely visible behind the verandas screened, as they are, by a wooden, cross-hatch. The ornamental, cast-iron fence which surrounds the property as well as the attractive, free-standing gazebo, south of the house, both dating to the turn of the century, suggest gentler and less hurried times.

J.R. Tantum, a homeopathic doctor, came to Winter Park from Wilmington, Delaware. In 1881 he was one of the very earliest purchasers of a lakefront lot from Chapman and Chase. His property occupied the northeast corner of Interlachen and New England Avenues on which the Langford Apartments now exist; this was immediately south of Judge Welborne's establishment. In 1883 Tantum built a home on his lot while residing at the Rogers House. This was a prime location from which to observe the horse-drawn "streetcar" as it brought patrons from the railroad station to the Seminole Hotel. Tantum was, indeed, briefly the President of the Winter Park Hotel Company.

Dr. Tantum passed away in 1887; in 1890 his residence was acquired by William Schultz, father of Walter and Arthur. With the building of the Langford Apartments in 1948, Tantum's cottage was moved northward so that it now lies between the Apartments and the Cloisters. At that time its lovely verandas were removed. Mr. and Mrs. James Crum from Michigan purchased it in 1952 and for twenty-five years rented the six apartments into which they divided it. It was the Crums who added the fancy ironwork to its facade and named the establishment "Lacy Shadows".

Tantum-Schultz Cottage (1883), NW corner Interlachen and New England replaced by Langford Apartments

"Lacey Shadows", formerly Dr. J.R. Tantum's Cottage, Interlachen Avenue

The **Wagner-Shannon cottage** at 173 Stovin Avenue is of interest for its association with Jean Wagner Shannon whose life we have profiled in an earlier section. A bungalow, it is at the opposite end of the spectrum from the grander Comstock, Temple or Geer-van den Berg houses; it is rather a simple, retirement bungalow. It does, however, enjoy a highly desirable, quiet location overlooking a portion of the Winter Park Golf course and its apparent simplicity belies its living qualities and value in the present-day Winter Park. (Refer photo page 69)

Likewise, the **Caldwell-Strong residence** at 155 Stovin is of greater interest for its association with the Caldwell and Strong families than it is as an architectural entity. When built by Dr. and Mrs. Campbell, Dean of Rollins Chapel, it was in very much the same idiom as its westerly neighbor (#173). The easterly wing, including a two car garage with living quarters above, is of course a more recent addition, so also that to the west. There is more living-space here than meets the eye; the location, within easy walking distance to the center of town, is superb. (photo page 70)

"The Palms" - the Brewer Mansion, located on the eastern shore of Lake Osceola, even today qualifies as one of the grandest residences in Winter Park. The property was originally owned by Alonzo W. Rollins. Upon his death in 1887, he willed it to the College. Its groves provided welcome income until the great freeze of 1895 when the citrus industry in Florida was virtually destroyed. At this point in time, Edward H. Brewer, a well-to-do manufacturer of carriage accessories from Cortland, New York came to Winter Park for his health. He purchased the former Rollins property from the College which was badly in need of operating funds, and in 1898 built a winter home on it. Although he suffered greatly from his illness, in 1923 at age 72, he undertook a vast modification of the house so as to have it duplicate, in appearance, his impressive Georgian Revival mansion in Cortland. As fortune would have it, he passed away on September 26, 1924 never having seen the transformation completed.

In 1937, the house was acquired by Mr. and Mrs. Frederick Detmar Trismen of Forest Hills, N. Y. who retained architect James Gamble Rogers II to redesign the interior. In 1951 Trismen sold 35 of the 40 acres in the original estate to Archibald Granville Bush who sub-divided it into Osceola Shores and Detmar Terrace. Upon Mr. Trismen's death in 1958 the house was acquired by Holland D. Thompson of Shaker Heights, Ohio; the Thompsons occupied it for ten years.

More recently, the Robert Govern family came into possession of this impressive, Georgian Revival residence. In 1982 Govern was convicted of trafficking in drugs; the house and all of its contents were confiscated by the Federal government. It has stood vacant ever since. Mayor Hope Strong proposed that it be acquired as a long needed home for the Winter Park Historical Association, but neighbors objected to this more intensive use of the property. Things being what they are in Winter Park, someone is sure to acquire this grand mansion and bring it back to its former glory. (The Brewer House is listed on the National Register of Historic Places)

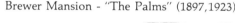

Brewer Mansion - "The Palms" (1897,1923)

"The Palms" - south facade of the great house

"The Palms" - alternate aspect of the facade

THE GEORGIAN REVIVAL IN WINTER PARK

The so-called Georgian Style is, in reality, an expression of Italian Renaissance architecture in Britain, introduced by Inigo Jones in the early 17th century. It attained its full flowering 150 years later, at mid 18th century, in the works of such men as James Gibbs and the Adams brothers. The style, widely emulated in the American colonies to the closing years of that century, (i.e. to 1800), is known as Georgian Colonial. Out-standing examples are found everywhere along the East coast - some of the best in Tidewater Virginia. It was succeeded by the Federal style (1795 - 1825) and a succession of Revival styles (Greek, Gothic, Romanesque) to the 1890's when, after a hundred years, a significant Revival of the Georgian Colonial style took place - particularly in the northeast and the midwest.

Brewer's home in Cortland, New York and the duplication of its facade at Winter Park, are expressions of this revival. Characteristic forms of the style are: a rectangular block often having an offset, pedimented pavilion projecting from the center of its principal facade (or a columned portico as in the case of "The Palms"), and corner pilasters. The hip roof was preferred; symmetry was the rule. Furthermore, great attention was given to the front entrance which might be embellished with a split-scroll pediment or, at the very least, a simple pediment. Above this, at the second floor level, there was frequently a Palladian window.

There are not many Georgian Revival residences in Winter Park due, in part, to the fact that its population was shrinking as a result of the great freeze of 1895, at the very time when the Revival was flourishing (1890 - 1915). One that has attracted our attention, is located at 253 Webster Avenue, at the corner of Golfview. It is painted buff with white trim. This house has the essential Georgian elements set forth above: it takes the form of a rectangular block; it has a hip roof (albeit extremely shallow in pitch), corner pilasters, a simple portico and total symmetry. The eaves brackets are, however, a discordant note - a carry over from the Victorian era of the 1870's and '80's. The eaves, therefore, are much broader than is typical, but represent a practical deviation providing a measure of shelter from the

E. R. Phillips'. Georgian Colonial Revival House at 253 Webster Avenue

"Cloister Groves". James Stokes House (1918), 1461 Via Tuscany

frequent showers and hot Florida sun. Our guess is that this house was constructed circa 1900-1910.

Another more typical Georgian Revival house, is located at 1461 Via Tuscany. Here, the interruption of the portal pediment and the string course by the single window above is a little disturbing. A Palladian window above the string course would not only have been faithful to the Georgian vocabulary, but more attractive as well. When this residence was built by James Stokes of Connecticut in 1918, it was surrounded by citrus groves and acres of lawn meticulously cared for.

Architect James Gamble Rogers' versatility is shown in that he designed at least two residences in the Georgian Revival style in Winter Park - the grandest of these, at 225 Palmer Avenue, opposite the north end of Old England, for Mrs. F.A. Mizener. The year was 1936. Rogers relates the following story about this commission:

"Mrs. Mizener was very shrewd and knew how to stretch a dollar and, I believe, was very successful with her investments. She wanted a Southern Colonial house but refused to go along with some of the characteristic adornments, and for the very practical reason of not having to paint shutters every year, refused to have them.

Laurence Hitt was job forman for this project in our office and as such had to be the one to pressure Mrs. Mizener into maintaining the integrity of the Colonial design. Mrs. Mizener was a very good sport and appreciated Laurence's suggestions, but was quite adamant about eliminating any "gym-cracks", as she called them, that were not structurally necessary or aesthetically essential. She came into the office quite regularly, as the preliminary drawings were progressing, with suggestions and minor changes which she would pencil out and leave with Mr. Hitt. He would check over these lists and incorporate the practical suggestions in the drawings. On one particular list that bothered Laurence more than usual, he noted along side of the items such phrases as "this won't work", "this is a silly idea", "she's going to ruin this house, damit, etc."

Later on, Mrs. Mizner asked the secretary to let her look up some letter she had written; the secretary gave her the file forgetting that Laurence's comments were in it. I do not recall that Mrs. Mizener said anything about these comments at the time, but several days later she came in with another list which she reviewed with Laurence. When they were through she started for the door, but stopped and said, "I forgot something". She came back to Laurence's table and at the bottom of her list of notes wrote, "Oh Hell!".

Mrs. Mizener paid $35,000 for her fine house in 1939.

The second of the two Georgian Colonial houses by Rogers, at the SE corner of Palmer and Old England, was designed in 1936-37 for Mrs. Steinway of the piano manufacturing family. It is a house which might be found anywhere in New England; its only adornment being the simple pediment over its entrance. Rogers certainly did not intend the aluminum awning.

Of course, the most obvious example of a Georgian Colonial building in Winter Park is its First Congregational Church (1924) designed by W. H. Nicklas of Cleveland, O. assisted by H. M. Reynolds of Orlando. This was built in the same block, as the original Gothic Church to which the Rev. Edward P. Hooker came in 1884, but is closer to Interlachen on which its principal facade fronts (the 1884 church faced New England Avenue). At first glance the Winter Park Church evokes the image of Bulfinch's First Church of Christ (1816-17) in Lancaster, Mass.; both have pedimented porches above which cupolas tower. However, this comparison cannot be carried further. There is little precedent for a Georgian Colonial Church in Winter Park, but then in 1924, the direction of Winter Park's architecture was quite fluid. It is none-the-less a handsome addition to the Winter Park scene and, stylistically, ties the community to its New England roots.

First Congregational Church (1924), Interlachen at New England Avenues

Georgian Colonial home of Mrs. F. A. Mizener (1936)

Steinway House (1936–37), corner Palmer and Old England Avenues (Charles Schmidt House).

Shades of New England - a Colonial House with pent roof at 876 Old England Avenue

Above - Pool and dock - Hauck-Bolen House, Isle of Sicily
Below - Lake Maitland viewed from Bush-Curry House

Above - Pool and gazebo, Holt-Mumby House
Below - Pool, Lake Maitland - from clubhouse - Alabama Condominium

MORE ON J. GAMBLE ROGERS II

Earlier we have discussed the influence of Gamble Rogers' French Provincial and Spanish Renaissance designs on the direction of domestic architecture in Winter Park commencing with the building of his own residence, "Four Winds", on the Isle of Sicily in the French mode (1929). (refer page 46) Another splendid expression of this Provincial style is seen at 711 Bonita Drive - across the way from "Eastbank" - the Comstock-Harris house.

Turning to his Spanish designs, there are some additional comments we would like to make regarding that best known, "Casa Feliz" - the Barbour house, at 656 N. Interlachen Avenue. Its walls are of solid brick, 12 inches thick, salvaged from an old Orlando Armory. The clay roof tiles, left over from the Florida boom of 1925, were found at Penney Farm in north Florida. These, formed over the human thigh, are said to have come from Barcelona to Cuba where they were traded by an enterprising American roof salesman for some standing-seam, tin roofing.

Other features of this house are its hand-made, Spanish wall-tile, its leaded bottle-end windows and hand made electric fixtures designed by the architect. It should be pointed out that additions have been made to the original design by succeeding occupants as family requirements demanded. Set far back from Interlachen Avenue on a large property bordering Lake Osceola, "Casa Feliz", is, indeed, one of Winter Park's most engaging residential conceptions.

The previously mentioned George Holt House (1936) at 1430 Elizabeth Drive overlooking Lake Osceola, includes many of the forms see at "Casa Feliz" - in particular its cantilevered balcony and its countrified Spanish character. There is a romantic, old-world quality about this design which makes it an "eye-stopper" - to use the architect's language - for any appreciative house-looker. (refer also page 49).

There is a Spanish, country house behind a head-high, stuccoed wall at 1290 North Park Avenue which might well have come from Roger's drawing board. In addition to the tell-tale, cantilevered balcony, its red-tiled roof has the same slope as that seen in the Holt House; furthermore, its

1290 Park Avenue North - a Spanish Renaissance design

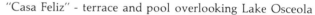

"Casa Feliz" - terrace and pool overlooking Lake Osceola

engaged chimney-pot and fenestration also exhibit similarities. If this house is, indeed, not attributable to Rogers, it certainly reflects his influence; it projects the same picturesque informality.

In 1933 Gamble Rogers was retained by Mr. Barbour, whose "Case Feliz" he had so recently completed, to design a number of apartments at the SE corner of Swoope and Knowles Aves. These derive their attractiveness from the recessions and progressions of their articulated facades; also from the subtle change in volume of their constituent parts. Note the exterior stair on the block closest to Swoope, which could well be the only one of its type in Winter Park, also the chimney-pots throughout.

There are several residences on Palmer Avenue east of the Osceola-Maitland canal by Rogers. While they possess his Spanish Renaissance vocabulary of forms, they are more formal than those considered thus far. That at #800, painted white with dark green shutters under a red tile roof, was built for C. A. Coddington. It is particularly impressive in its meticulously landscaped setting. Another nearby, identified as "Merrywood" at #1020 - its Spanish buff stucco contrasting with its red tile roof - was designed by Rogers for a Mrs. Plant from Boston in 1938. Upon viewing a contemporary photo of this house, the architect denied having carried out the appendage with round-headed windows at its west end. (refer to overleaf)

The residence at 950 Palmer Avenue, for some years occupied by the Schencks, was built by Joshua C. Chase, father of Cecelia Chase Lasbury, in 1926. It, too, is in a Spanish buff color under a red tile roof. The house displays all the romantic characteristics observed in Rogers designs, but the date is a little early and we cannot confirm its attribution to him - in face have no reason to believe that he designed it. (The same may be said for the house next-door at 966 Palmer Avenue which has been occupied by the Battaglias since 1956.) Mrs. Chase was a good friend of Hamilton Holt's wife who answered to the name of "Zeenie". Since Mrs. Chase liked to entertain and had great fun doing so, she often invited the Holts and their distinguished guests to dinner - among these, on one occasion, the architect of Knowles Memorial Chapel - Ralph Adams Cram.

711 Bonita Drive - French Provincial by James Gamble Rogers II

The Barbour Apartments (1933), Knowles and Swope Avenues

Built for C.A. Coddington (1941)-James Gamble Rogers II, architect

Chase-Schenck House (1926), 950 Palmer Ave.

"Merrywood" (c.1938), 1020 Palmer Avenue, built for Mrs. Caroline Griggs

The Beckwith-Battaglia House, 966 Palmer Ave., pastel green stucco with red tile roof

ARCHIBALD GRANVILLE BUSH

Many well-to-do people have been attracted to Winter Park over the years, but none wealthier or more generous in their philanthropies than Archibald Granville Bush and his wife, Edyth Bassler Bush. Bush's life is the typical Horatio Alger story. He was born on a 240 acre farm in Granite Falls, Minn. in 1887. In 1908 he attended the Duluth Business College. The following year, at age twenty-two, he became an assistant bookkeeper at the 3M Company (Minnesota Mining & Manufacturing) with which firm he was associated for the next fifty-seven years until his death in 1966. In 1921 he was elected to its Board of Directors; then in 1949 became Chairman of the Executive Committee of the Board. Thirty years earlier, in 1919 at age 32, he had married Edyth Bassler of Chicago - a beautiful, aspiring, young actress.

The author is not certain when the A. G. Bushs commenced spending their winters in Winter Park, but it surely was well before 1952 for, by that time, he had developed a keen interest in the affairs of Rollins College and had become a trustee. Ten months before his death, during the Presidency of Hugh F. McKean, Bush made a munificent gift of $800,000 towards the $3.5 million cost of the Archibald Granville Bush Science Center on campus. Earlier he had given $50,000 towards the establishment of the Roy E. Crummer School of Business Administration. Upon his death in 1966 his estate was valued at over $100 million.

Mrs. Bush's estate of $71 million was the largest ever filed in Orange County to that time (1972-73). In 1966 she had established the Edyth Bush Charitable Foundation, the headquarters for which - originally in Minneapolis - were moved to Winter Park following her demise. Since that time, the Foundation has dispersed and/or otherwise appropriated over $25,000,000 to various, needy charitable, educational, health services and cultural organizations, chiefly in Central Florida, including, of course, the Edyth Bush Theatre at Lock Haven Park, Orlando.

The impressive Bush mansion and grounds known as "Twelve Oaks", located at 1200 N. Park Avenue on Lake

Archibald Granville Bush (1887 - 1966)   Edyth Bassler Bush (18??-1972)

Maitland, were valued at $1 Million in 1973. Although the approach to the home continues to be imposing, a portion of the original grounds - adjacent to Lake Maitland - have been developed as a cul de sac which includes the residence of former Senator Paula Hawkins among others. (Refer to pages 99-100 for a description of the Bush house interior)

Winter Park has been very fortunate in that so many of those who have come her way and who could afford to, have given generously to the betterment of the community and the college. Archibald Granville Bush and Edyth Bassler Bush were such persons.

Martin Hall (c.1923), a Mediterranean villa on Lake Virginia. Built as Business Men's club.

Martin Hall - the commodious center hall

FIVE OUTSTANDING WINTER PARK HOMES

MARTIN HALL

If one word were to be used to describe Martin Hall, that would would be impressive. The Hall was originally built in the early 1920's by a group of Winter Park businessmen to serve as headquarters for a Business Men's Club. R. F. Hotard was the Club's first president, Arthur Schultz the initial vice president. The Business Mens Club's occupancy was comparatively short-lived for the club-house was purchased by W. R. Rynlander of Orlando in 1925 for $85,000. Rynlander, in turn, sold it to John and Prestonia Martin in March of 1930. With the assistance of Sam Stoltz, an interior designer, the Martins remodeled and restored the property as their home.

Dr. Martin came to Winter Park and to Rollins College at the invitation of Pres. Hamilton Holt; he had been a contributor to Holt's publication, *The Independent*. A native of Lincolnshire, England, Martin was a friend of George Bernard Shaw and, like Shaw, embraced the Socialist tenets of the Fabian Society. He also befriended such men as Ramsay McDonald, H. G. Wells and Maxim Gorky. His wife, the former Prestonia Mann - daughter of a prominent New York physician who associated with Ralph Waldo Emerson and Walt Whitman - was related to Horace Mann, the educator.

At Rollins Dr. Martin was a conference leader and a consultant on International Relations. His lectures were so popular in the community and by Rollins students, that they were often transferred to the Congregational Church. Imagine two such power-houses as John Martin and Hamilton Holt in the small Rollins community at one-and-the-same time for a period of twenty years!

Martin Hall, as the Mediterranean mansion became known following his death in 1956 when it was acquired by Rollins and placed in service as its Conservatory of Music, is ambassadorial; from all reports, the Martins had furnishings befitting it. It is located on the east shore of Lake Virginia opposite the College; as one enters Genius Drive, it is the first habitation encountered behind a low wall and cast-iron gate through which one gains access. Three elongated windows, topped by colorful, semi-circular panels with Adamesque designs, accent the entrance pavilion.

Within, one immediately enters a great stair-hall which extends from a solarium on the lakefront facade through the full width of the structure. Standing in the center of this hall, one looks east to the great stair framed by a stunning pair of convolute columns. The entrance to the grand parlor to one's right is similarly framed, likewise that to the spacious dining-room across the hall. There are then six, in all, of these marvelous columns with composite capitals. Both dining-room and parlor have stately fireplaces; that in the former, manorial in concept, is of sculptured stone, that in the parlor has an over-mantel fully seven feet tall supported by engaged, volute columns which frame a decorative, ceramic panel. 'Spacious' is the word applicable to these ground-floor rooms.

The western end of this grand hall leads to a commodious, glass-enclosed sun-room or solarium from which one gains access to a terrace and lakefront garden affording splendid vistas across Lake Virginia. A plaque on this western facade reads as follows:

"This house and its grounds are dedicated to the memory of Prestonia Mann Martin (1862-1945), wife of John Martin. Her memory and spirit continue always to bless it."

'Beautiful' is still another word descriptive of Martin Hall, Winter Park's most stately mansion, and the sentiment expressed above by its distinguished, longtime occupant. The College relinguished its ownership of the mansion during a poor real estate market in the 1970's; since, it has been in private hands.

Martin Hall - parlor viewed from center hall

Martin Hall - hall and entrance to solarium viewed from dining-room

Martin Hall - the solarium

THE RIPPLES ESTATE

The original Ripples house - Ripples I - was built in 1910 by the Hon. Isaac Hopper. Within three years it came into the possession of a Mr. J. C. Stineman who, in 1922, sold the property to Mr. and Mrs. Walter Randall of Cincinnati, Ohio. It was the Randalls who built the impressive Mediterranean mansion which we see today, said to have been designed by a leading New York architect (James Gamble Rogers name is mentioned) at a cost of $180,000 - an extremely high price for a home at that time. The great house, located on Spring Lane overlooking Lake Sue at the southern extremity of Winter Park, was one of the largest in Central Florida when built in 1923. It was considered to be a masterpiece of design and construction; its walls are of poured, reinforced concrete eighteen inches thick; its large rooms enjoyed an incomparable view across the lake.

Martin Hall - view from the lakefront terrace

Martin Hall - dining-room viewed from the center hall

Its high 13′ ceilings and many windows served as a built-in air-conditioning system. The windows were an innovation in that those in the dining-room lowered into the basement; the second-floor bedroom windows opened into the ceiling-thereby allowing both elements of the double-hung windows to be opened. The house contained six large fireplaces - each one unique. Floors in the drawing-room, dining-room, hallways and enclosed porches were of Rookwood tile in differing designs and borders. The Rookwood Pottery in Cincinnati, Ohio, with which the Randalls were, of course, quite familiar, was a leading manufactory of art nouveau ceramics at the turn of the century.

Rookwood tiles, designed by daughter, Laura Randall, elsewhere enhanced the interior decor. Mrs. Randall designed an exquisite wrought-iron gate leading to the dining-room, also a weeping willow fountain set into the wall of the largest porch. Water dripped from the willows' branches into a sunken pool. The lighting fixtures were of original designs. There are many other refinements throughout this distinctive mansion which the Randalls occupied for almost thirty years to 1952.

In 1960 the property was purchased by Mr. and Mrs. Richard E. Webb for a reported $50,000; Mr. Webb was the owner of the Northside Drug on Fairbanks Avenue in Winter Park. Immediately following its purchase the Webbs are said to have undertaken a complete remodeling of it. However, they soon sold the house to the Mormon Church who used it as a retreat. Acquired by the Maxwell Stitts in 1972, still another change in ownership in 1975 brought it into the appreciative hands of Dr. and Mrs. Alphonso Sainz who, once again, restored it. (It is to be hoped that these several "restorations" have not compromised the original beauty of the interior). A movie, "The Meal", no credit to itself or to Winter Park, was filmed in the mansion immediately before its occupation by the Sainzes. The "Ripples" was a "Designer Showcase House" in 1982.

"The Ripples" (1923) - Spring Lane, the Walter Randall Mansion

"Casa Feliz" - Lake Osceola viewed from terrace

THE HAMILTON HOLT HOUSE

Readers of this book will know by now that the author, in the course of researching it, developed a profound respect and admiration for Hamilton Holt, President of Rollins College between 1925 and 1949. His longtime residence, therefore becomes, for him (i.e. the author), something of a shrine. The house, located at #208 Interlachen Avenue almost opposite Osceola Lodge, was built by Mrs. S. F. Pryor in 1922. It was acquired by Rollins ten years later, in 1932, as a home for its President.

It occupies a large property extending from Interlachen to Lake Osceola's shore and is approached by a long driveway. The front entrance admits one to a wood paneled hall which leads directly into the living-room oriented in a north-south axis. This inviting room has a beamed ceiling and a fireplace on its inside wall. It was here that President Holt entertained students, over the years, singly and in groups. Without doubt, it was in this room, also, that he received many of the distinguished visitors he brought to the College in connection with "The Animated Magazine", the granting of honorary degrees and other functions. With a little imagination, one can still sense his presence. There is a very large family-room at the north end of this parlor.

Following Holt's retirement in 1949, the house served as an off-campus residence hall, a sorority house, a museum of art and, in 1969, for a period of five years, as the chancellor's office. It was purchased by Dr. and Mrs. Mumby in 1979. The new owners have added a lovely terrace and free-form swimming pool complete with a picturesque gazebo, altogether affording one of the most rewarding lake views in all of Winter Park.

Holt-Mumby House - pool, gazebo and Lake Osceola viewed from terrace

The Holt-Mumby House (1922), 208 Interlachen Avenue, Osceola facade with pool in foreground

98

"TWELVE OAKS" - THE ARCHIBALD GRANVILLE BUSH ESTATE

In an earlier chapter we have profiled the lives of Archibald Granville Bush and his wife, Edyth Bush. The Bushs certainly commenced coming to Winter Park before 1952 for, in that year, he became a trustee of Rollins College. In that year, also, Edward F. Keezel, whose very desirable property bordering North Park Avenue Bush purchased, passed away while in retirement at Ashville, N. C.. This estate, combined with the beautiful, adjacent Irving Bacheller property, comprised the original Bush holdings.

Built in 1956 at a cost of $150,000, the Bush house is more contemporary than others which we have considered; so contemporary, in fact, that it is difficult to believe that it was constructed over a third of a century ago. The only departure from contemporary decor within was Mrs. Bush's bedroom suite which incorporated French Provincial moldings and cornices to blend with her furniture. The house is virtually fireproof; all partitioning is of masonry, steel joists support the green glazed tile roof. The exterior walls are of stucco-coated, hollow, clay tile in combination with native, northern stone. Belatedly, the author has learned that James Gamble Rogers II was Mr. Bush's architect. It is somewhat suprising that in personal meetings with Mr. Rogers, his involvement with this project was never mentioned, nor has it been included in photographic exhibits of Mr. Rogers work (Cornell Fine Arts Center, Rollins College, April 13 - May 8, 1985; Maitland Art Center, December 15, 1985 - January 12, 1986). It may be that Mr. Rogers served as resident architect.

A long, private driveway at 1200 North Park Avenue winds through the estate to the porte-cochere proceeding the front entrance. An unusually gracious hall extends from this entrance, through the width of the house to a large solarium over-looking Lake Maitland. The large parlor or living-room, at left, is entered through a wide opening of the hall so that the latter virtually becomes an extension of the it. The hall, the parlor and the formal dining-room beyond, all have the same light, cream-colored, marble flooring which serves to integrate as well as to enrich the entire area and to

make of it a marvelous space for entertaining sizeable groups. The living-room, extending from front to rear, is illumined by large windows at either end and, at night, by indirect lighting. This is a truly elegant interior space and, as Frank Lloyd Wright and others have declared, - space is the essence of a building.

Archibald Granville Bush House (1956), the porte-cochere

Irving Bacheller Cottage - demolished to make way for A. G. Bush House

Archibald Granville Bush House - entrance hall viewed from the living-room

Archibald Granville Bush House - Living room viewed from the entrance hall

Archibald Granville Bush House - the formal dining-room

Archibald Granville Bush House - the solarium overlooks Lake Maitland

THE MacCAUGHEY-TAYLOR HOUSE

The MacCaughey-Taylor residence is located at 1411 Via Tuscany directly opposite the Annie Russell residence. Its appearance suggests that it is a house with a history, not one built in the post World War II era. Its white, stucco exterior finish glistens-intensified by the bright Florida sun. The brilliant blue of Lake Maitland is glimpsed through the breezeway connecting the main house with guest and/or servants quarters. No small part of its visual charm derives from its asymmetry and the varied roof lines of its several component parts. (refer also to color-plate page 71)

We knocked at the breezeway entrance, seeking permission only to photograph Lake Maitland from the vantage point of this property, but unexpectedly, were invited to view the interior. Beyond the kitchen and formal dining-room one glimpses the parlor's cathedral ceiling from the resplendent, polygonal entrance hall which, with its several rounded-headed doorways, acts as a distribution center; the latter's soffits encircle panels bearing unusual, decorative cartouches.

This living-room, perhaps better referred to as a 'hall', is elegant in every respect. Its floor, as well as that of the entrance hall and dining-room, is paved with pale, red clay tile - pointed at either end. Its walls are of richly striated travertine marble; the woodwork is of distressed, native pine. The furnishings are quite in keeping with the majesty of the architecture.

"Many of the decorative elements, including particularly the great, stone fireplace and mantle are said to have been acquired from Addison Mizner of Palm Beach" the mistress declared - pointing to a photograph of a Mizner interior in which the hearth was duplicated. "They do not build them like this any more; incidentally, this house is Mediterranean in style, not Spannish".

Andrew Bonner MacCaughey, who built this refined residence circa 1925, was a well-to-do Chicago businessman. He was born in Cobury, Ontario in 1875 and passed away in this home in June of 1945 at the age of seventy; however, not before having enjoyed twenty winters in Winter Park. No doubt there are many other architectural surprises in Winter Park where the exterior hardly suggests the living space and the refinement within.

The MacCaughey-Taylor House (c. 1925), 1411 Via Tuscany

MacCaughey-Taylor House - Lake Maitland viewed from

101

MacCaughey-Taylor House - the parlor, cathedral ceiling

MacCaughey-Taylor House - the polygonal entrance hall

THE BRITTANY HOUSES

The so-called "Brittany Houses" on Via Lugano immediately west of its intersection with Via Tuscany are of interest. These articulated residences are characterized by low profile, broad, low-sloping, shingled roofs, by banded windows and attractive, round-headed chimney pots, but particularly by dove-cotes under gable ends facing the road. They constitute a unique, but welcome stylistic deviation from the many fine, contemporary homes in the immediate neighborhood.

Brittany House - unique architecture at the corner of Via Tuscany and Via Lugano

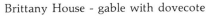

Brittany House - gable with dovecote

Charles Hyde Pratt House - 1551 Via Tuscany - International style in an unlikely place

103

SOME CONTEMPORARY RESIDENCES

"Sevilla" - an enclave of contemporary homes

"Quo Vadis" 719 Kiwi Circle - an impressive Winter Park contemporary

"Schoet Elkote" - Bermuda style on the Isle of Sicily

C215 Salvador Square, Sevilla district

255 Sterling Drive - an impressive contemporary design fronting on Lake Virginia

The Royer House (c.1975), 704 Kiwi Circle, by James Gamble Rogers II

Walker Residence (1948), 279 Virginia Drive - overlooks Lake Virginia attributed to James Gamble Rogers (unconfirmed)

King residence (1938), 458 Virginia Drive. Although this house has elsewhere been attributed to James Gamble Rogers, he denies having designed it.

Gen. Brereton House, 960 Keyes Avenue - stately design overlooks Winter Park golf course

331 Beloit Avenue (c. 1978) - one of a series of row houses by Ashington-Peckett

"Quoins" - at the corner of Palmer Avenue and Anchorage Court

Above - 'Casa Feliz' - entrance court - Interlachen Ave.
Below - "Windsong" - Genius Drive

Above - Rose Garden, Central Park
Below - Scene on Genius Drive

The Osceola-Maitland (Venetian) Canal

Scenic Boat Tour Dock, at the foot of Morse Boulevard

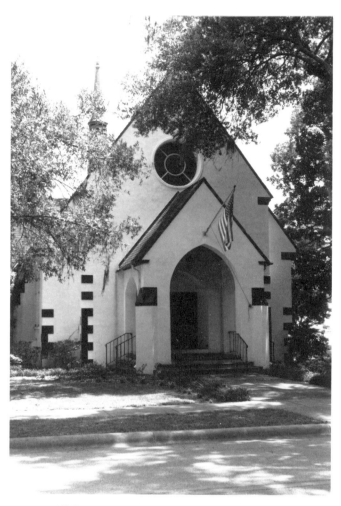

All Saints Episcopal Church (founded 1886)

The Colony and Park Plaza Hotel, Park Avenue

The Langford Hotel (1956), New England Ave. at Interlachen

Winter Park Post Office - 32789

Winter Park City Hall, Park Avenue at Lyman

EPILOGUE

What would Chapman and Chase think if they could return to Winter Park today? They would, of course, be astonished by the traffic everywhere in town, also by the paved roads and sidewalks. They would not recognize a single building on Park Avenue although the original commercial building which they erected at the corner of the Boulevard, and the Pioneer Store at Welborne, still exist - hidden behind their brick veneers. They would look with wondrous eyes at the new (1924) Congregational Church to which, as New Englanders, they would relate. They would be astonished and pleased by the development of the Rollins campus - still possessing one building, Pinehurst Hall, which they would remember.

They would take great pride in the fact that the plan which they adopted for Winter Park has worked so well - that the Central Park has been respected, that Interlachen Avenue and the Boulevard are there just as they planned them, that Winter Park is a city of homes beyond their fondest dreams. They would know a few of these which have endured over the intervening century: - William Comstock's "Eastbank", Dr. Guild's establishment, Dr. Geer's cottage, also that of the Rev. G. M. Ward. They would be dismayed that the vast groves, the open spaces and the tall pines are no more. They would be amazed that these once large tracts have been broken up so that there is hardly a foot of lakefront property without a house on it. Property values would astound them. "We surely knew a good thing when we saw it!", they might exclaim to each other.

If, after being shown around they sat down on one of Central Park's benches and collected their wits, if they took note of its rose garden, its fountains, the brick planters lining its sidewalk, the great live-oaks and the character of the commercial facades across the way; if they reflected on the beautiful homes they had just seen on Via Tuscany, Palmer Ave., Kiwi Circle, Virginia Drive and Sevilla, I think they would like Winter Park and congratulate themselves. In many ways, considering the lush semi-tropical vegetation which has been introduced, the azaleas everywhere in spring - not to mention air-conditioning, Winter Park is a more beautiful and livable place today than it was 100 years ago.

Relaxing in Central Park

Central Park during the 1987 Art Festival

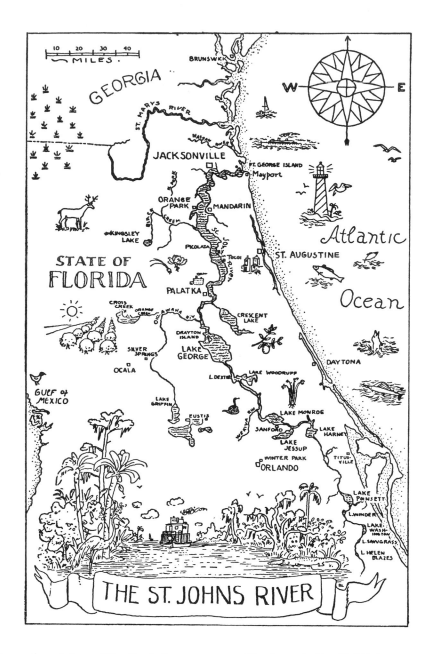

Reproduced from *The St. Johns*, courtesy Rinehart & Co. Publishers

BIBLIOGRAPHY

A HISTORY OF FLORIDA by Carlton Teabeau, University of Miami Press, 1971.

HISTORY OF ORANGE COUNTY by William J. Blackman, E. O. Painter, Publishers, 1927.

ROLLINS COLLEGE - A PICTORIAL HISTORY by Jack Lane, Rollins College, Publisher.

FACTS ABOUT FLORIDA IN GENERAL AND WINTER PARK, Winter Park Improvement Association, 1890.

ARCHIVES - OLIN LIBRARY, Rollins College, Numerous booklets, photographs and manuscripts.

LOST TREASURES OF LOUIS COMFORT TIFFANY by Hugh F. McKean, Doubleday & Co., 1980.

HISTORIC WINTER PARK - A DRIVING TOUR published by the Junior League of Orlando-Winter Park, 1980.

TALES OF WINTER PARK - Edited by Hope Strong Jr. Rollins Press, Publishers, 1982.

HISTORICAL ASSOCIATION PRESENTATION by Harold and Betty Ward - on file Winter Park Public Library 11/20/74.

WINTER PARK SCRAPBOOK, compiled by Loring Chase, 1882 - 1906. Edited and indexed by Dorothy Shepherd Smith - 3 volumes.

CARVING HIS OWN DESTINY; THE STORY OF ALBIN POLASEK by Ruth Sherwood, 1954. Ralph Fletcher Seymour, Publisher, Chicago.

THE FIRST CONGREGATIONAL CHURCH OF WINTER PARK, FLORIDA by Harry S. Douglas, 1987.